Sailing as a
Second Language

Sailing
as a
Second Language

An Illustrated Dictionary

The Seamanship Series

Fred Edwards

International Marine Publishing Company
Camden, Maine

Published by International Marine Publishing Co.,
    a division of Highmark Publishing Ltd.,
    P.O. Box 220, Camden, Maine 04843.

Typeset by Camden Type 'n Graphics, Camden, ME
Printed and bound by Bookcrafters, Chelsea, MI

Line illustrations by Jim Sollers
Illustration on page 62 courtesy Richard Henderson

10   9   8   7   6   5   4   3   2   1

Library of Congress Cataloging-in-Publication Data

Edwards, Fred.
    Sailing as a second language.

    (The Seamanship series)
    1. Sailing—Dictionaries.   I. Title.   II. Series.
GV811.E35   1988   797.1'24'0321   88-1623
ISBN 0-87742-965-0

To Pauline—
sailor, wife, friend, sweetheart.

Preface

For years, each time I needed a definition or a spelling for a sailing term, I had to search through nautical dictionaries, instructional books, old sailing ship glossaries, Navy manuals, general dictionaries, and the dozens of nautical catalogs that sailors collect. One day I realized that sailors needed a one-volume sailing dictionary for practical use. And to be practical it had to be the right size.

It needed to be big enough to contain most terms a sailor might use and hear during a daysail or a cruise. A pamphlet saying essentially, "Port is left and starboard is right," just wouldn't do the job.

Yet it had to be small enough in size and content to be useful aboard the boat. An eight-pound dictionary chock full of square-rigger and clipper ship terms is no help to a sailor in a modern fiberglass sloop wanting to recall quickly the difference between a No. 1 genoa and a No. 2.

Finally, it had to be organized so that a sailor could find the information needed. This meant cross-referencing, of course, but it also meant that, for example, when a sailor forgot the name for a forward spring line, he should have a place to look other than "forward spring line."

I started the book with enough knowledge to be opinionated (show me a sailor who isn't)—knowledge acquired through years of sailing, teaching sailing, and writing about sailing. I needed every bit of this experience, plus all the reference materials mentioned earlier (and a host more), to get this encyclopedic dictionary underway. Webster's Third New International Dictionary complicated matters, because many spellings disagreed with the other sources. However, I went with Webster when possible, while including other commonly used spellings.

Anybody with the audacity to claim he knows enough about sailing to write a dictionary about it is setting himself up for a heap of criticism if he makes errors. That's the chance I had to take in order to fill the need for this type of book. Please send your suggestions to the publisher. In order to improve the next edition of *Sailing as a Second Language,* I will correct any outright errors and will give careful consideration to all other comments.

Fair winds and calm seas . . . and good sailing!

Introduction

Yes, sailing *is* a second language. Sure, you might go out for a day of instruction and begin sailing right away, but how would you answer a friend in another boat who shouted something like: "Drop your small Danforth, and I'll raft up on your starboard side for lunch. Put a fender midships and be prepared to receive bow and stern lines. Watch the spreaders, and have a couple of springs ready."

Or what if you're explaining a dolphin striker to a group of aspiring sailors, and one says, "My Uncle Harry said that was a martingale"?

These terms, and more than 800 others, are explained in this encyclopedic dictionary. Because it is not a multi-volume set, a great deal of information important to a sailor's education had to be excluded. If you are a dedicated sailor (and there is hardly any other kind), I encourage you to ensure that your sailing library ashore includes all sailing subjects in detail.

Meanwhile, here is *Sailing as a Second Language* to use as a quick reference afloat and ashore.

Definitions are arranged in alphabetical order by word. When entries have the same first word, alphabetical order is determined by the second word, etc., and all two-word entries are completed before proceeding to the next single-word alphabetical entry. Thus all entries beginning with **anchor** as a separate word, are placed before **anchorage**. Hyphenated words are treated as two separate words. This is the system generally used by telephone directories.

If a main word has more than one spelling, or a definition applies to more than one word, the secondary word is placed in parentheses following the main word. Primary and secondary words, as well as directive references to other primary words, are in all boldface. Cross-references are also in boldface.

Let's hope the book makes sailing a second language for *you*.

a

aback (backwinded)   When a headsail has its clew to windward, instead of the normal position to leeward. This may occur due to a sudden change in wind direction or be done on purpose when heaving-to. See **heave-to.**

wind

This boat has its jib aback.

abaft   Toward the stern of the boat. Behind.

abeam   At right angles to the centerline and outside the boat.

aboard   On or within the boat.

about   (With "go" or "come"), to put the boat on the opposite tack.

above decks   On the weather deck. Opposite of **below.**

abreast   Side by side. Same as **abeam.**

accommodation ladder   Portable flight of steps down the side of a large vessel.

adrift   Not made fast to any stationary object. Not moving under its own power.

aft   An adverb meaning toward the stern of the boat.

after   An adjective meaning toward the stern.

aground (on the ground, on the bottom)   A boat goes aground when she draws more water than is under her keel.

ahead   In the direction of and forward of the bow.

ahoy   Hello. Also used to call attention.

ahull   Said of a boat that is drifting with all its sails furled.

aid to navigation   A man-made object that supplements natural landmarks in indicating safe and unsafe waters.

alee   Away from the direction of the wind. To **leeward.**

all hands   The entire crew.

aloft   Above the weather deck. Overhead. Up the mast. In the rigging.

alongside   Beside.

amidships (amidship, midships)   The middle portion of a boat between the bow and the stern, or between port and starboard. Also the centered position of the rudder.

anchor   An anchor and **rode** (line and/or chain) secures the boat to the sea bed. The rode is attached to a **shackle,** or ring, at one end of the **shank. Flukes** for digging in are at the opposite end (**crown**). Tips of the flukes are called **bills.** A **stock** assists in positioning the flukes.

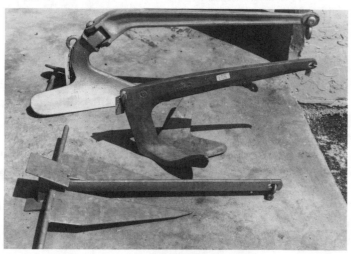

flukes

shank

crown

stock

Anchor parts

Burying anchors, such as the Bruce, CQR (plow), Danforth, mushroom, and Wishbone, hold well on soft bottoms. Bruces and plows hold well on most bottoms except hard rock. Hooking anchors, such as the Northill and kedge (yachtsman's), can penetrate hard bottoms and grass, weeds, or kelp. See **anchoring.**

Anchors. From front to rear: Danforth, Bruce, Plow.

anchor bend (fisherman's bend)   See **knots and splices.**
anchor light   See **riding light.**
anchor watch   Person standing watch on an anchored vessel.
anchorage   An area where it is safe to anchor because of water
   depth, good holding ground, and shelter from wind
   and seas.
anchoring   **Scope** is the ratio of **rode** (line and/or chain) to
   water depth, and varies with boat size, the amount of
   chain used, and weather conditions. A scope of 7:1 to
   10:1 is generally indicated for heavy weather.

   A boat can be anchored with either a **bower** (an
   anchor carried at the bow) or (not fully accepted) a
   stern anchor. If the anchorage is crowded and wind and
   current are not expected to change, setting both bow
   and stern anchors can be effective. For strong varying
   currents in crowded anchorages, a **Bahamian moor**
   (two bow anchors 180 degrees apart) is indicated. A
   Mediterranean moor, popular in European waters, is
   accomplished by setting a bow anchor and backing up
   to a quay.

   In strong winds a **fork moor** (two bow anchors
   about 45 degrees apart) provides extra safety. Shack-
   ling one anchor behind another with a single chain

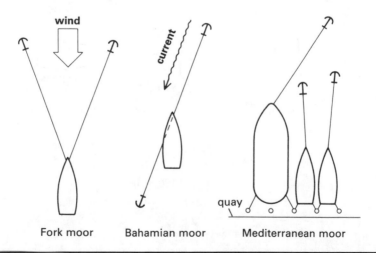

Fork moor   Bahamian moor   Mediterranean moor

3

running crown-to-shank (tandem anchors, sometimes known as **backing an anchor**) can provide tremendous holding power.

A **riding weight** can be shackled to the rode and lowered to increase horizontal pull. A **trip line** (also called a tripping line) attached to the crown and secured to an anchor buoy (float) before anchoring can be used to raise a fouled anchor.

Anchors and anchoring techniques are covered in detail in *Anchoring* by Brian M. Fagan, a volume in the International Marine Seamanship Series. See also **sea anchor.**

anemometer A device that measures the wind's velocity. It can be fitted to the masthead and connected to an instrument panel in the cockpit, or it can be a self-contained, hand-held unit.

angle on the bow The angle of your boat's bearing from another vessel, measured from his bow either port or starboard from 0 through 180 degrees.

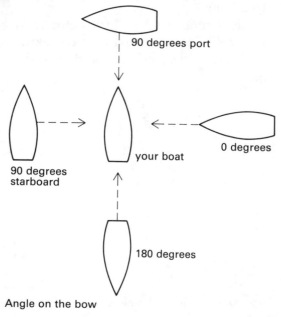

90 degrees port

90 degrees starboard

your boat

0 degrees

180 degrees

Angle on the bow

antenna   Wire or whip used for radio communications, generally connected to the radio by a cable.

anti-fouling paint   See **bottom paint.**

apparent wind   See **wind.**

arm   To put tallow into the cavity of the lead on the end of a lead line in order to get samples of the bottom when sounding.

ashore   On shore.

aspect ratio   The ratio between the luff length and the foot length of a sail. A **high aspect ratio** refers to a tall, narrow sail, while a **low aspect ratio** refers to a low, broad sail.

High aspect ratio

Low aspect ratio

astern   In the direction of and beyond the stern. Opposite of **ahead.**

athwart (athwartships)   At right angles to the centerline of the boat.

automatic pilot   An electro-mechanical steering device with a compass, which when set and coupled to the boat's steering system, maintains the boat on a constant compass course.

auxiliary   A sailboat's engine. A sailboat with an auxiliary engine.

avast   Stop!

awash   At or near water level, or inundated. Also a rock, reef, or submerged object whose upper part breaks the surface of the water.

aweigh The position of the anchor when it clears the bottom during hoisting.

awning A canopy to protect against sun and weather.

azimuth An object's direction measured as an angle clockwise from true or magnetic north. See **compass.**

back A sail is backed when it is moved to windward of the centerline, in order to slow the boat. See also **wind.**

backing an anchor See **anchoring.**

backstay See **standing rigging.**

backwash Water thrown aft by the turning of a vessel's propeller.

backwinded When wind is deflected from one sail to the leeward side of another sail, as when the jib backwinds the main. See **aback.**

baggywrinkle (bagywrinkle) Anti-chafe material placed on the shrouds to protect the mainsail.

Baggywrinkles

Bahamian moor See **anchoring.**

bail To remove water with a bucket or similar container. The instrument used to remove the water is a **bailer.** Also a metal loop fastened to a spar, to which a fitting can be attached, such as when fastening a boom vang to the boom.

This bail is used to attach a vang to the boom.

6

bailer   See **bail.**
ball cock   See **through-hull fitting.**
ballast   Weight placed low in the boat or on the keel to give stability.
ballast-displacement ratio   The ratio of ballast to the total displacement of the boat, a measure of stability. The minimum for traditionally designed cruising boats is generally 30–40 percent. Racing boats may have over 50 percent.
bar   A bank or shoal, such as a sand bar.
barber hauler   A line or tackle attached to a jib sheet between the clew and the fairlead, used to adjust the sheeting angle.
bare poles, sailing under   Sailing without any sails set. Generally running before heavy wind.
barge   A cargo-transferring boat usually with no self-propulsion capability. Also a warship's boat for flag officers.
bark   See **sailing rigs.**
barkentine   See **sailing rigs.**
barnacles   Hard-shelled sea growth on bottoms of boats, piers, etc.
barometer   An instrument which measures atmospheric pressure and helps in forecasting weather.

Barometer

batten   See **sail parts.**
batten down   To secure or tie down fittings, such as hatches, in preparation for heavy weather.
beach, on the   Ashore or on land.
beacon   A navigational aid. A **radio beacon** is identified by Morse signal and provides a line of position when using a radio direction finder. A **light beacon** is identified by color and light characteristics. See **light characteristics, line of position.**
beam   The width of the boat at its widest point.
beam ends, on her   When a boat has rolled 90 degrees (so that her deck beams are vertical).

beam reach   Sailing with the apparent wind coming at right angles to the boat.

bear   To lie in a certain direction from the observer. Also to sail in an indicated direction.

bear a hand   Lend a helping hand. Make haste.

bear away (bear off)   To alter course away from the wind.

bear down   To approach from windward.

bearing   The direction of one object from another, measured in degrees from true or magnetic north, or measured relative to the centerline of the observer's boat. See **compass.**

beating   Sailing to windward. Close-hauled. By the wind. To reach an objective to windward.

Beaufort scale   A table that correlates wind speeds with wave heights and other visual phenomena to describe the strength of the wind. The scale ranges from Force 0, a flat calm, to Force 12, a hurricane. See table on opposite page.

becalmed   No wind.

becket   A looped line, hook and eye, strap, or grommet used for holding lines, spars, or oars in position.

becket hitch   See **knots and splices.**

before the wind   Running. Sailing in the same direction as the wind.

belay   To make fast a line to a cleat or belaying pin. Also, to stop or to cancel, or to order to stop or cancel.

belaying pin   A rod or pin used in making running rigging fast.

bells   The half-hours of a four-hour watch are announced by bells, beginning with one bell, e.g. 0030, and ending with eight bells, e.g. 0400.

below (below decks)   Under, down. Opposite of **above decks.**

bend (bend on)   To secure one thing to another, as to bend a flag onto a halyard, or to attach a sail to its spar. See also **knots and splices.**

Bermuda rig (also Bermudian)   See **sailing rigs.**

Beaufort number or force	Wind speed (knots)	Description	Effect offshore
		Beaufort Scale	
0	under 1	Calm	Sea like a mirror.
1	1–3	Light air	Small ripples, like fish scales.
2	4–6	Light breeze	Short, small pronounced wavelets with no crests.
3	7–10	Gentle breeze	Large wavelets (2 feet) with some crests.
4	11–16	Moderate breeze	Small waves (4 feet) becoming longer, with some whitecaps (foam crests).
5	17–21	Fresh breeze	Moderate lengthening waves (6 feet), with many whitecaps, and chance of spray.
6	22–27	Strong breeze	Large waves (10 feet), extensive whitecaps, some spray.
7	28–33	Near gale	Sea heaps up; white foam from breaking waves (14 feet) begins to be blown in streaks.
8	34–40	Gale	Moderately high waves (18 feet) of greater length, edges of crests break into spindrift (heavy spray), foam is blown in well-marked streaks.
9	41–47	Strong gale	High waves (23 feet), dense foam streaks, crests begin to roll over, spray reduces visibility.
10	48–55	Storm	Very high waves (29 feet) with long overhanging crests, sea begins to look white, visibility is greatly reduced, rolling of the sea becomes heavy and shocklike.
11	56–63	Violent storm	Exceptionally high waves (37 feet) that may obscure medium-sized ships, all wave crests blown into froth, sea covered with white patches of foam.
12	64 & up	Hurricane	Air filled with foam and spray, waves 45 feet and over, sea completely white.

Bernoulli's Principle   See **slot effect.**

berth   A bed or bunk. Also a position for a vessel at a dock or an anchorage.

bight   A bend or loop in a line. Also a relatively open bay or cove.

bilge   The lower part of a vessel where waste water and seepage collect. Bilge water is the accumulation of such liquids. Also the sectional shape of the hull below the waterline.

bilge keels   Shallow keels placed on either side of the centerline to provide lateral resistance and stability. When the tidal range is so great that the seabed is exposed at low tide, a boat can rest upright on her bilge keels.

Binnacle

bilged   When the bilge has been staved in.

bills   See **anchor.**

binnacle   A stand or pedestal for holding the compass.

binnacle list   The sick list, excused from duty. In olden days it was posted on or near the binnacle.

bitter end   See **knots and splices.**

bitts   Strong posts on a pier or quay for securing lines, often called **bollards.** Also small posts fixed through the deck to which the bowsprit is attached or to which docklines are made fast. **Quarter bitts** are on the quarters and are often used to secure a dinghy painter or a towline. **Towing bitts,** as on a towboat, are very strong and placed some distance forward of the stern.

Bitt

blanket   To deprive the sail of the wind by interposing another object.

block   Nautical term for pulley. A wooden or metal shell (whose sides are called **cheeks**) enclosing one or more **sheaves** (grooved wheels) through which a line may be passed, and having a hook, eye, or strap by which it may be attached to a surface such as a spar or deck. Two blocks with a line through them form a **tackle**.

Block used as a turning block, to change the direction of a line.

blower   A rotating fan for circulating air.

boat   A sailboat, rowboat, or yacht. (*Naval terminology:* a vessel that can be carried on a ship.)

boathook   A staff with a hook and prod at one end, used to fend off, to hold on, and to pick up lines and moorings.

A boathook is useful for catching pilings, lines, or in this case, a finger pier.

boatswain   (pronounced **"bosun"**) See bos'n.

bobstay   A stay from the lower stem (bow) of the boat to the end of the bowsprit that counteracts the upward pull of the forestay. The bobstay may be held down at a more advantageous angle by a spar from the bowsprit perpendicular to the bobstay, called a **martingale** or **dolphin striker.**

Bobstay. Note the dolphin striker projecting down from the bow.

bold shore   A steep, rocky shore with deep water close to it.
bollard   See **bitts.**
boltrope   A reinforcing rope along the foot or luff of a sail.
boom   A spar to which the foot of a sail is attached. Also a crane aboard a vessel used for handling cargo.
boom crotch (boom crutch)   A notched board or X-shaped frame that supports the main boom when the sail is lowered. See **topping lift.**
boom preventer   See **preventer.**
boom vang   A device (usually a tackle) secured to the boom to prevent it from lifting, reducing the risk of an accidental jibe and providing better sail shape when sailing off the wind. See also **preventer.**
boomkin   See **bumpkin.**

boot stripe (boottop)   A line on a hull, painted just above and indicating the designed waterline.

bos'n (bosun, correctly spelled boatswain)   In the Navy, an officer or petty officer in charge of deck work. The deck foreman.

bos'n's chair   A portable seat suspended from a line, by which a person can be hoisted up the mast.

bos'n's locker   A place where deck gear is stowed.

bos'n's pipe   A small, shrill silver whistle used by a bos'n's mate to pass information.

bottlescrew   See **turnbuckle**.

bottom   The part of the boat below the water line. Depending on their general shape, boats may be flat-bottomed, vee-bottomed, or round-bottomed. Also the sea bed.

bottom paint   Paint used on the bottom, usually of a chemical make-up that resists marine growth, called **anti-fouling paint**.

bow   The forward (front) end of the boat.

bow line   A docking line at the bow.

bow pulpit   See **pulpit**.

bow roller   A roller fairlead over which rode and chain travels when an anchor is lowered or raised.

bow wave   Wave caused by the motion of the bow through the water.

bower   See **anchoring**.

bowline   See **knots and splices**.

bowsprit   A spar that projects from the bow and extends the sail plan by allowing headsails to be secured forward of the bow.

break out   To unpack or prepare for use. Also, to free an anchor from the bottom.

breaker   A wave whose crest topples over in foam when the wave becomes unstable due to excessive height or running over shoal bottom. Of obvious danger to vessels. Also a small water cask.

breaking seas   See **seas**.

breakwater A structure used to break the force of waves.

breast line See **docklines.**

bridge deck On a sailboat, a raised deck between the cockpit and the companionway that prevents water in the cockpit from spilling into the cabin.

Bridge deck

bridle A span of line with both ends secured. Used when towing a boat or when being towed. Also used with a tackle when lifting heavy objects.

brig See **sailing rigs.**

brigantine See **sailing rigs.**

brightwork All varnished woodwork and polished fittings, especially topside.

Bristol fashion Neat, clean, in good condition. Shipshape.

broach When a boat turns broadside to the waves, subjecting it to possible capsizing. Generally occurs when running.

broad on the beam At right angles to the beam and outside the boat. Abeam.

broad on the bow A direction midway between abeam and dead ahead.

broad on the quarter A direction midway between abeam and dead astern.

broad reach Sailing with the apparent wind coming over either quarter.

brow See **gangplank.**

bulkhead A vertical partition across the boat that strengthens and/or divides the hull.

bulwark A parapet around the deck of a boat that prevents gear from falling overboard and protects the decks from the sea.

bumboat A small boat used in ports to sell merchandise.

bumper See **fender.**

bumpkin (bumkin, boomkin)   A spar projecting over a boat's stern or side, similar to a bowsprit. A bumpkin projecting from the stern may be used to attach a fixed backstay.

bung   A stopper (usually wooden) used to plug holes, such as a screw-hole, or a leaking end of a malfunctioning through-hull closure system.

bunk   A built-in bed.

bunk board   See **leeboard**.

bunt   See **reefing**.

bunting   A collection of flags, or the material from which they are made.

buoy   A floating aid to navigation which is anchored to the bottom. Buoys may be lighted, with specific identifying characteristics, or unlighted. They may be silent, or may contain whistles, fog horns, or bells. Red **nun buoys**, which are tubular with conical tops and have even numbers, are normally found in American waters on the starboard hand when entering a channel from seaward. Green (formerly black) **can buoys**, which are tubular with flat tops and have odd numbers, are normally to port. Buoys of varying colors and sizes are used for other purposes. See **daymark, light characteristics.**

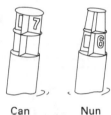

Can   Nun

buoyancy   The floating quality of a boat.

burdened vessel   See **give-way vessel**.

burgee   A small triangular or swallow-tailed flag normally used to identify the yacht club of which the boat owner is a member. Flown at the top of the mast or at the starboard spreader.

butterfly   See **wing and wing**.

Buys Ballot's Law   See **wind**.

by the lee Sailing on a run with the wind blowing from the leeward side (the same side as the boom). This can cause an accidental jibe.

wind

by the wind Sailing close-hauled, beating.

This boat is sailing by the lee. An accidental jibe may result.

C

cabin An enclosed living space in a boat.

cable The anchor rode. Olden measurement of 100 fathoms.

camber The curve of a sail. The convex curve of the deck from one side of the boat to the other.

cam cleat See **cleat.**

can buoy See **buoy.**

canoe stern See **double-ender.**

capsize (turn turtle) To turn over, so that the mast is upside down in the water. Also sometimes used to describe a small centerboard boat that has suffered a knockdown from which it cannot self-right. See also **knockdown.**

capstan (windlass) A drum with a vertical axis around which an anchor rode is wound, to give mechanical advantage when raising or lowering a heavy anchor. A capstan may be hand operated or power driven.

This capstan unit is located farther aft than on larger boats. Its handle (nearly vertical) is removable.

captain (skipper)   The person aboard a boat with ultimate authority and responsibility.

careen   To heel a boat over, generally on a beach, for hull maintenance or repair.

carry away   To break free. See also **part.**

carvel   Smooth-planked. For illustration see **lapstrake.**

cask   A wooden barrel used to store liquids.

cast off   To let go.

cat rig   Rig of a catboat. See **sailing rigs.**

cat's paw   A light current of air on the surface of the water.

catamaran   A twin-hulled boat with hulls side-by-side.

catboat   See **sailing rigs.**

catch a crab   To immerse an oar accidentally during the recovery stroke, thus losing control.

catwalk   See **finger pier.**

caulk (calk)   To fill the seams of a boat with fiber or compound to make it watertight.

celestial navigation   A method of navigation based upon the observer's location relative to pre-calculated positions of a heavenly body. The navigator measures the body's altitude with a **sextant.** By comparing that altitude and location against a known altitude and location selected from the tables, he can plot a **line of position.**

centerboard   A wooden or metal board that can be raised and lowered through a trunk and slot in the bottom of the boat to reduce leeway. See also **daggerboard.**

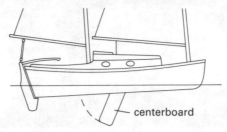

centerboard

centerline   The center of the boat on a fore-and-aft line.

center of effort (CE)   The center of wind pressure on a sail, or on the combination of all sails being carried on a boat. Placing the CE above the center of lateral resistance (CLR) balances the helm. Moving it forward produces a lee helm; aft produces a weather helm. The CE is moved forward (to correct for weather helm) by hardening in the jib sheet, tightening the cunningham, luffing the main, or reefing the main. It is moved aft (to correct for lee helm) by hardening in the main-

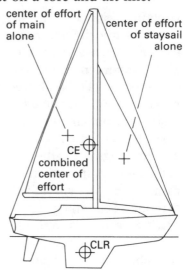

With the center of effort (CE) approximately above the center of lateral resistance (CLR), the helm is balanced. Because the CLR does not move, balance must be maintained by adjusting the CE.

sheet, reducing the size of the headsail, or raking the mast aft. See **center of lateral resistance.**

center of lateral resistance (CLR) The center of underwater sideways resistance, approximately the center of the underwater profile. The point around which the boat will turn. The CLR can be moved aft (to correct for weather helm) by partly raising the centerboard, or in small boats by moving live ballast aft. See **center of effort.**

chafe To wear by rubbing. See **chafing gear.**

chafing gear Sacrificial coverings such as canvas, rubber, plastic, or small stuff (light cordage, yarn, or line), used to prevent chafe. See also **fender.**

chain locker Compartment for stowing anchor rode.

This chain locker, located in the forepeak, contains rode for two bow anchors. One is secured to the bowsprit, the other to the starboard side of the bow pulpit. Coiled line (upper right) is *not* part of the ground tackle.

Chainplates, external. Often attached internally.

chainplate A metal fitting made fast to the side of a sailboat, to which a shroud or stay is attached.

chart   A map for use by mariners, which depicts water depths
and bottom materials; heights of overhead obstructions; aids and hazards to navigation; details of shore-
lines, ports, and harbors; geographical coordinates;
and more. In the United States, the standard navigational charts are the NOAA charts, published by the
U.S. Department of Commerce.

The scale is a fraction, such as 1/5,000, which indicates that one unit on the chart equals 5,000 units on
the ground or water. A **small-scale chart,** with smaller
fractions (such as 1/250,000), shows more area in less
detail, whereas a **large-scale chart** (such as 1/20,000)
depicts less area in greater detail.

A chart created by **mercator projection** produces
parallel lines of latitude, and a course plotted thereon
as a straight line will be a **rhumb line.** A chart with
gnomonic projection produces straight lines of longitude radiating from the nearest pole, and curved lines
of latitude, resulting in a course plotted as a straight
line being a **great circle.** See also **geographic coordinates.**

check valve   A valve, such as in an overboard discharge line,
that lets water out but prevents water from entering.

cheek   See **block.**

cheek block   A block whose sheave is mounted against a spar
or other surface.

chine   The angle of intersection of the topside and the bottom.
The more abrupt the angle, the harder the chine.

chip log   See **speed logs.**

chock   A U-shaped fairlead used for mooring and anchor
lines.

chord   An imaginary line between the luff and leech of a sail,
parallel to the foot.

chute   Slang term for spinnaker, derived from the old term,
parachute spinnaker, which was coined when double-
luff spinnakers first evolved.

clam cleat   See **cleat.**

class   General category into which boats of the same or similar design are grouped.

claw off   To work off, close-hauled, from a lee shore.

claw ring   A C-shaped fitting that is slipped over the boom, for example, when the sail has been roller-reefed, to allow the boom vang to be reattached.

cleat   A fitting to which lines are made fast. A **horn cleat** is the classic, anvil-shaped cleat with horizontal arms around which a line is made fast. A **cam cleat** holds a line by jaws that work on a moving cam. A **clam cleat** has two immobile jaws. A **jam cleat** has one horn formed to make a line fast quickly by friction.

A midship horn cleat

clevis pin   See **toggle.**

clew   See **sail parts.**

clew outhaul   See **running rigging.**

clinometer   Device that measures the degree of roll, heel, or list.

close aboard   Quite near to a vessel.

close-hauled   Sailing as close to the wind as possible. Beating, on the wind, or by the wind.

Clinometer. The bubble in the tube (below) shows the angle of heel.

close reach   Sailing with the sheets eased slightly, and the apparent wind forward of the beam.

clove hitch   See **knots and splices.**

club-footed   A club-footed headsail's foot is made fast to a spar that swings freely forward of the mast.

coaming   A vertical piece around a deck opening or cockpit to prevent water on the deck from running below.

cockpit   The well in a boat's deck from which the vessel is manned.

coffee grinder   A large, powerful sheet winch, mounted on a separate pedestal, with two handles that rotate about a horizontal spindle. Used often in maxi-boat racing.

coil   To lay down line in circular turns for stowage.

collar   A vertical piece around a mast hole in a deck to help make the joint between deck and mast watertight. See also **mast coat.**

collision mat   Any heavy, mattress-like object used to plug a hole in the hull.

COLREGS   See **Rules of the Road.**

come about   To bring the boat from one tack to the other when sailing by the wind, or close-hauled. Coming about brings the bow through the eye of the wind. See **jibe.**

commissioning   Placing the boat in operation.

committee boat   The boat from which race officials direct a race.

companionway   (**companionway hatch**)   Opening leading from the deck down into the cabin.

This companionway has a raised sill, which reduces the risk of downflooding if the cockpit ships a sea.

companionway ladder   The steps leading from the deck to the cabin. Located in the companionway hatch.

compartment   A space enclosed by bulkheads, deck or sole, and overhead. Similar to a room in a house.

compass   An instrument used to indicate direction relative to the earth's magnetic field. Its **azimuths,** or **bearings,** are designated on a compass card by degrees or points measured from magnetic north. (See **points.**) Large vessels have a gyro compass, indicating true north.

compass

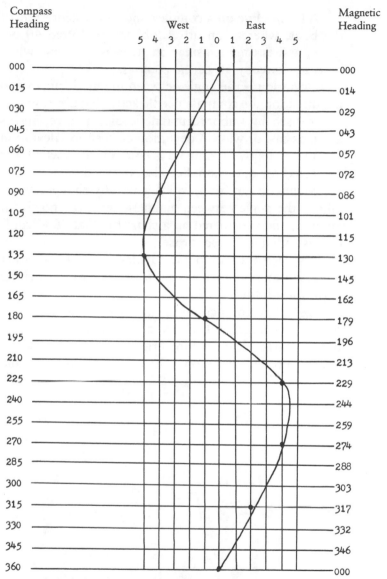

A deviation card can be prepared from a deviation curve, which is derived from swinging compass through eight or more bearings. Although the top half of the deviation curve will seldom match the bottom half exactly, a badly skewed curve indicates a poorly compensated compass or inaccurate readings while swinging compass.

23

compass

A **lubber line** on a compass shows the centerline of
the boat, whereas an offset lubber line (often 40 degrees) assists the helmsman in steering a course when
he is not directly aft of the compass.

Deviation is the angle between magnetic north and
the direction the compass needle actually points, generally caused by onboard magnetic disturbance, and is
given as east or west. A deviation card shows deviation
for all headings. A compass is **compensated** when it is
corrected for deviation. See also **swing ship.**

Magnetic variation, which generally changes annually, is the angle between magnetic and true north for
an area, and is depicted on a chart by dual 360-degree
circles called a **compass rose.**

An electronic compass provides a reading in either
digital or analog (meter-type) form. It requires neither
card nor a lubber line.

Details of compass usage are covered in *Sailing in
the Fog* by Roger F. Duncan, a volume in the International Marine Seamanship Series.

compass rose   Printed circles on a chart representing true and

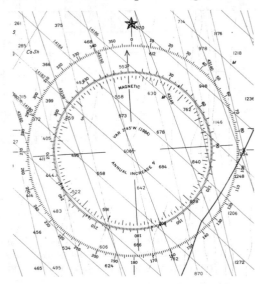

Compass rose

24

magnetic compasses, showing variation and annual change in variation for that area. Used to determine the direction of a course or bearing.

compensate   See **compass.**

compression post   A vertical post placed between the foot of a deck-mounted mast and the keel.

cordage   A general term for all types of rope.

cotter pin   See **toggle.**

cotter ring   See **toggle.**

counter   The underside of the after overhang of the vessel.

counter

course   The direction (magnetic or true) steered or made good by a vessel. **Course through the water** is course steered. **Course over the ground** is the actual course made good after incurring the effects of leeway and current.

courtesy flag   A miniature of a foreign country's national ensign, flown at the starboard spreader while in that country's waters.

cove stripe   An ornamental, painted or grooved, fore-and-aft band on the hull, usually close to the sheerline.

cow's tail   See **fag end.**

cradle   A frame that supports a boat when out of water.

craft   See **vessel.**

cringle   A ring sewn into a sail through which a line can be passed, usually at each corner of the sail. See **reef cringle.**

cross-trees   See **spreaders.**
crown   See **anchor.**
crutch (crotch)   See **boom crutch.**
cuddy   A shelter cabin in a small boat.
cunningham   A cringle and line in the luff of a sail above the tack, which allows tightening of luff tension during strong winds, thus flattening the sail.
current   The horizontal movement of water, caused by tide or wind, or both. See **tidal current.**
cutlass bearing   See **shaft.**
cutter   See **sailing rigs.**

D=ST (D=RT)   Distance equals Speed (Rate) X Time. Basic formula for calculating distance run, boatspeed through the water, or elapsed time. Knowing any two factors makes it possible to calculate the third. See **dead reckoning.**
daggerboard (dagger plate)   A board in the center of the boat that can be raised or lowered vertically. When lowered, it performs as a keel does, reducing leeway. See also **centerboard.**
davits   Mechanical arms extending over the side or stern of a vessel, or over a sea wall, to lift a smaller boat or other weight.

Davits supporting a dinghy at the stern.

daymark An aid to navigation near shore which can be seen during daylight hours. In channels leading from seaward, red triangular daymarks with even numbers generally mark the starboard side, while green rectangular daymarks with odd numbers mark the port. When traveling the Intracoastal Waterway, from New Jersey through Texas, triangles are normally to starboard and squares to port. See **buoy.**

daysailer An open boat used for day sailing.

dead ahead Directly ahead of the vessel's bow, or directly on the vessel course.

dead astern Opposite of **dead ahead.**

dead in the water A vessel underway that is making neither headway nor sternway.

dead reckoning (deduced reckoning, ded. reckoning, DR) A method of navigation whereby a position is plotted based upon speed, elapsed time, and the course steered from a known position (fix). Intermediate plots are **estimated positions** (EPs), which may be supplemented by lines of position (LOPs). A DR cycle ends when a new position, or fix, is determined. If the vessel makes leeway, or is set by current, the course and speed through the water will differ from its **track,** which is the course and speed over the ground (course and speed made good). See **fix, line of position, reciprocal bearing, running fix.**

deadrise   The vertical distance between the top of the keel of a vessel and the turn of the bilge. The upward slope of a vessel's bottom. See **turn of the bilge.**

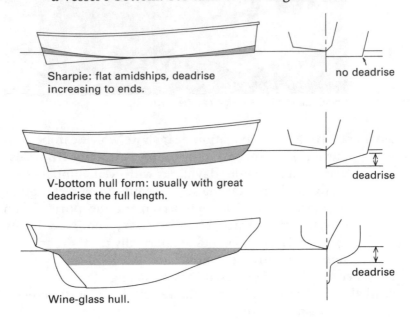

Sharpie: flat amidships, deadrise increasing to ends.

no deadrise

V-bottom hull form: usually with great deadrise the full length.

deadrise

Wine-glass hull.

deadrise

deck   A permanent covering over a compartment or a hull. See also **bridge deck.**

deck horse   See **running rigging.**

deck sweeper   A genoa with foot cut to ride along the foredeck.

deckhouse   Structure built on a weather deck which does not extend over the full breadth of the vessel. Can function as the "roof," and to some extent the "sides," of a cabin below.

deep six   To dispose of by throwing over the side.

depthsounder (depth finder, fathometer)   A device that measures water depth by means of a transducer, which times the sending of a sound pulse and receipt of its echo from the bottom.

deviation   See **compass.**

dew point   Temperature at which moist air becomes saturated and releases the water as droplets (fog). Dew point temperature varies with the amount of water vapor in the air (relative humidity). See **sling psychrometer.**

dinghy   A small open boat, often used as a tender for a larger vessel.

dink   Slang for a dinghy.

dismast   To carry away the mast of a boat.

displacement   The weight of water displaced by a boat. If it equals the weight of the boat, the boat floats.

displacement hull   A type of hull that plows through the water, displacing a weight of water equal to its own weight, even when more power is added. See **hull speed.**

Displacement hull   Planing hull

ditty bag   A sewing kit, consisting of sailor's palm, needles, thread, etc., used for repairing sails and similar items. Also a bag for personal articles. See photo on next page.

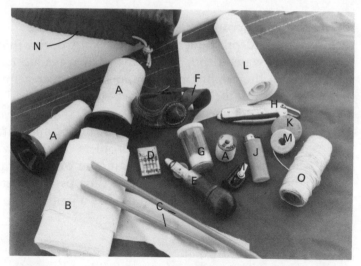

Sample contents of a ditty bag: A) three sizes of sail thread; B) old sail material; C) fids for splicing braided rope; D) sewing machine needles for sail material; E) hand stitching awl for tabling and leather; F) sailmaker's palm, right hand; G) hand sewing needles in container, protected by cotton and lubricant; H) rigging knife, with marlinespike; I) spare sail slide; J) cigarette lighter to fuse ends of twine or rope, preventing fraying; K) beeswax; L) sail cloth; M) waxed twine; N) the ditty bag; O) nylon twine for whipping.

dividers A navigational instrument consisting of a pair of arms that can be separated at one end to measure distances on a chart or plotting sheet.

dock A pier, wharf, quay, or other man-made platform where a vessel can be moored. Also the waterway extending between two piers. Also a verb meaning to moor at such a place.

docklines Lines used to make a boat fast to a dock or to another boat, identified by their location on the boat and their purpose. Bow and stern lines lead forward and aft respectively, and hold the boat alongside. **Spring lines** are generally longer, preventing the boat from moving forward or aft, while allowing it to rise and fall with the tide. A forward spring leads forward to the dock, preventing rearward movement. An after spring is the opposite. A spring line can also provide leverage for moving the boat into or away from the dock. **Breast lines** are led at right angles to the centerline of the boat to hold it against the dock.

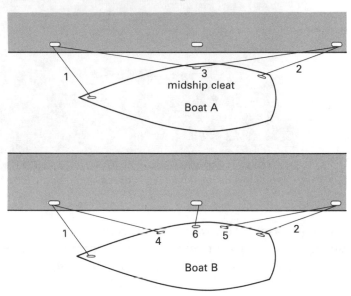

Docklines. Each boat has bow and stern lines (1 and 2). Boat A is also double-sprung, with forward and after springs running from a midship cleat (3). Boat B has a forward bowspring (4), an after quarter spring (5), and a breast line (6).

dodger   A screen fitted to protect the cockpit from wind and spray.

dog house (doghouse)   A low deckhouse.

dolphin   A group of piles driven close together and bound with wire cable into a single structure. Also a mooring buoy or spar resembling such a structure.

dolphin striker   See **bobstay**.

dorade ventilator   A deck ventilator designed to admit air but not water, first used on a boat named *Dorade*.

double-ender (canoe stern) A boat with a pointed bow and
stern.

Photo of this double-ender explains the origin of the term "canoe
stern."

douse (dowse) To lower sails quickly.
down by the stern (or by the head) Describes a boat whose
stern (or bow) is riding below the designed waterline.

Down by the head.

downhaul   See **running rigging.**
downwind   To leeward, away from the wind.
DR   See **dead reckoning.**
draft   The vertical distance from a boat's waterline to its lowest part.

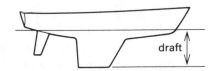

draw   A sail draws when it is filled by the wind. A boat with a four-foot draft draws four feet, i.e., it requires at least four feet of water beneath the waterline to prevent grounding. See **draft.**
drift   See **tidal current.**
drifter (flasher)   A large, lightweight headsail (3/4-ounce to 1-ounce material) that is made fast to the headstay or forestay by its luff. Its area is generally over 170 percent of the foretriangle and is used in light winds.
drogue   A device streamed astern to reduce a vessel's speed, or to keep its stern at right angles to the waves in a following sea. See also **sea anchor.**
dropboards   See **washboards.**
Dutchman's log   See **speed logs.**

earing (**earring**) A line attached to the cringle of a sail by which it is bent or reefed.

ease To slacken or relieve tension on a line.

ebb tide A receding, horizontal flow of tidal current.

electrolysis The chemical reaction between two dissimilar metals immersed in sea water, generally resulting in a gradual destruction of one. Counteracted by using similar metals, or if that is not feasible, by using sacrificial metal, such as zinc, which deteriorates instead of the boat's underwater metal fittings.

ensign A national flag of a boat's country of registration, flown at the stern. The horizontal dimension is the **fly;** the vertical edge, the corners of which are made fast to the flag halyard, is the **hoist.**

EPIRB Emergency Position-Indicating Radio Beacon, which when activated transmits an emergency signal on pre-set frequencies to aircraft and satellites, or to VHF radio receivers, depending upon type.

equal interval light See **light characteristics.**

estimated position See **dead reckoning.**

even keel When a boat is floating on its designed waterline.

eye of the wind The direction from which the wind is blowing.

eye splice See **knots and splices.**

fag end (cow's tail)   Frayed or untwisted end of a line.

fair   Said of a boat's hull to indicate she has no bumps or strange curves. Also, said of the lead of a line, such as a jibsheet, to indicate it is correct. Also, said of current or tide when it is running in the same direction as the boat's course. Opposite of **foul.**

fairlead   A fitting used to guide a line in the direction required.

fairway   Main channel in restricted waters down which boats should proceed.

fake   See **fake down.**

fake down   Coiling a line so that each coil, or **fake,** overlaps the one beneath, leaving the line free to run. See also **flake down.**

fall   The part of a tackle which is hauled upon.

fall off   See **head off.**

fancywork   Ornamental rope work.

fast   Secure, such as to make a line fast to a cleat.

fathom   Six feet, measured vertically below the surface of the water.

fathometer   See **depthsounder.**

favor   To stay close to, such as to favor the starboard side of a channel.

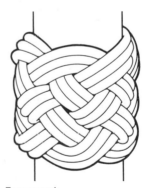

Fancywork

feather   To turn the blade of an oar or paddle horizontally at the finish of a stroke.

feel the way   Proceed cautiously, taking soundings or minding the depthsounder.

fend off   To push off the boat from an object that could chafe.

fender   A cushion-like device placed between a boat and a pier, or another boat, to prevent chafing. Often called a **bumper**.

Fender

fetch   When beating to windward, to make a windward mark without another tack. Also the distance through which a wave or wind system travels.

fiberglass   Glass-reinforced polyester of which most modern sailboats are constructed.

fid   See **marlinespike.**

fiddle   A rack or rail on the edge of a stove, table, etc., to keep items in place during heavy weather.

fiddle block   See **handy-billy.**

fife rail   A rail around a mast, at its foot, bored with holes to take belaying pins.

figure eight knot   See **knots and splices.**

fin keel   A ballasted keel centrally attached to the bottom of the hull, with a small fore-and-aft length relative to the boat's length.

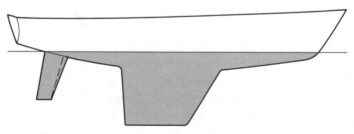

Fin keel with balanced spade rudder

finger pier (catwalk)   A narrow pier extending alongside a slip to parallel a docked boat.

fisherman's bend   See **knots and splices.**

fix   A confirmed location of the boat, determined by crossing two or more lines of position (LOPs), observing known objects, or other methods. See **dead reckoning, line of position.**

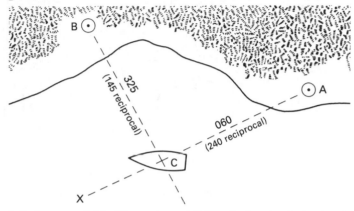

A fix from two LOPs. The reciprocal (240°) of a bearing to the tower at A (60°) supplies LOP A–X. The reciprocal (145°) of a bearing to the cupola at B (325°) supplies a crossing LOP, establishing a fix, C, which is the boat's location.

fixed light   See **light characteristics.**

flag officer   An officer in the Navy, the Coast Guard, or a boating organization who is authorized to fly his flag of office, such as an admiral or the commodore of a yacht club.

flake down   To lay line in figure eights so that it will run without kinking or fouling. Also a method of placing a sail in accordion-like layers across a spar when furling.

flare The outward curve of a vessel's sides. Opposite of **tumblehome**. Also a distress signal.

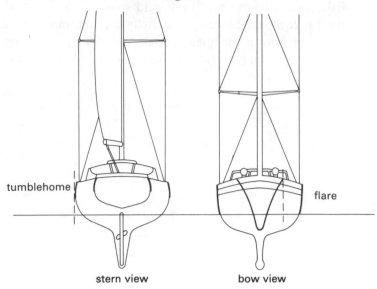

tumblehome flare

stern view   bow view

flasher See **drifter.**
flashing light See **light characteristics.**
flatten in To trim sails more tightly.
flemish To coil the slack end of a line in a continuous flat spiral starting with its bitter end in the center. Used for painters, docklines, etc.

Flemish

flood tide See **tidal current.**
flotsam Floating wreckage of a vessel or its cargo.
flukes See **anchor.**
fly See **ensign.**
following sea A sea which is traveling in the same direction as the boat. Opposite of **head sea.**
foot The lower edge of a sail or lower end of a mast. Also, to move through the water when sailing close-hauled.

fore-and-aft   In line from bow to stern. Parallel to the center-line. See **sailing rigs.**

forecastle (fo'c's'le)   The cabin farthest forward. On large vessels the crew's quarters forward.

forefoot   The heel of the stem where it connects to the keel. The forward extremity of a full keel.

foremast   On a schooner or square-rigger, the first mast abaft the bow.

forepeak   A compartment in the most forward part of the boat.

forereaching   The forward motion of a boat that is luffing while in the process of coming about, or that is hove-to.

foresail   In a schooner, the sail set from the foremast.

forestay   See **standing rigging.**

foretriangle   The triangular space enclosed by the forestay, the mast, and the deck.

fork moor   See **anchoring.**

forward   Toward the bow.

foul   To entangle, obstruct, or jam. A fouled anchor has its cable twisted around it, or in another sense, is jammed under an obstruction on the bottom. A line led the wrong side of something is said to be led foul. Also used with current or tide to indicate it is running in an opposing direction to the boat's course. Also, said of a boat's bottom supporting marine growth, such as barnacles.

foul-weather gear   Slickers, boots, sou'westers, and other such protective clothing for use onboard in the rain.

found   Equipped. A well-found vessel is well equipped.

founder   To sink.

fractional rig   See **standing rigging.**

frames   Structural members running athwartships and following the curve of the hull, to which planking is attached. Sometimes called **ribs.**

freeboard   The portion of a boat's hull above the waterline.

Boat on the left has more freeboard than boat on the right.

freshen   To prevent chafe by hauling in or slacking off a line. To freshen the nip of an anchor rode is to increase or decrease scope to prevent chafe. Also said of a wind that is increasing in strength.

full   Said of a sail that is full of wind. Opposite of **luffing.**

full and by   Close-hauled, with all sails full.

furl   To roll up a lowered sail and secure it. Also, to haul in on a roller-furling sail.

furling lines   See **sail stops.**

gaff   A spar that extends the head of a four-sided, fore-and-aft mainsail. See **sailing rigs.**

gale   See **storm warnings.**

galley   Where the cooking is done.

gallows frame   Raised thwartships structure to hold up a boom.

gangplank (brow, gangway)   Temporary bridge between the boat and the pier.

gaskets   See **sail stops.**

gate valve   See **through-hull fitting.**

gear   Equipment, clothing, tools, ropes, blocks, etc.

genny   A genoa jib.

genoa   A headsail that extends aft of the mast, thus being larger than the foretriangle. Genoas are sized by the formula LP/J x 100% = % genoa, where LP = genoa girth (a perpendicular from luff to clew) and J = length of the foretriangle base. A No. 1 genoa is generally from 170 to 200 percent. A No. 2 is 135 to 150 percent (75–80 percent of No. 1). A No. 3 is generally a 110-percent **lapper** (75–80 percent of No. 2).

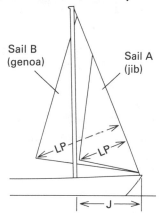

LP/J x 100% = % genoa. On sail A, LP is less than J, resulting in about an 80-percent jib. On sail B, LP is more than J, resulting in about a 140-percent, or No. 2 genoa.

genoa track   Fore-and-aft track on which sheet blocks are fastened.

geographic coordinates   Imaginary lines circling the earth horizontally and vertically, the intersections of which can identify a vessel's location. **Latitude** lines run east-west, paralleling the equator, and are measured north and south from the equator, from 0 to 90 degrees. **Longitude** lines are great circles that run through the poles, thus pointing to true north, and are measured from the **Greenwich (Prime) Meridian** east and west to

180 degrees, which approximates the International Date Line.

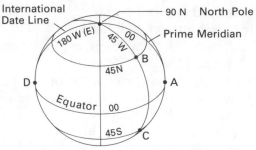

Geographic coordinates. Point A: 00 degrees, 00 degrees; Point B: 45 degrees N, 45 degrees W; Point C: 45 degrees S, 45 degrees W; Point D: 00 degrees N, 180 degrees W (or E).

ghosting   Sailing in almost no wind.

gilguy   Line to hold a halyard away from a mast so that it won't slap the mast annoyingly when at anchor.

gimbals   A system to suspend an object so that it remains horizontal when a boat rolls or heels.

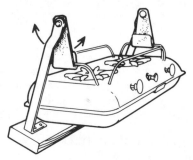

Stove mounted on gimbals, allowing it to swing as the boat heels.

give-way vessel   Under **Rules of the Road,** the vessel that must give way to the **stand-on vessel.** Formerly called **burdened vessel.**

gnomonic projection   See **chart.**

go about   See **come about.**

gooseneck A universal joint that secures the boom to the mast.

Gooseneck (center) attaches boom (right) to mast (left), allowing boom to move up-and-down and left-and-right.

goosewinged Said of a sail in the middle of a jibe that has its upper and lower halves on opposite jibes.

grabrail A handhold on a boat.

gradient wind See **wind.**

granny knot See **knots and splices.**

grapnel Small anchor with several hooks, used for dragging for lost objects, and sometimes for freeing a cable trapped under the anchor line of a later arriving boat.

great circle An imaginary line such as the equator, which is traced on the surface of the earth by a plane cutting

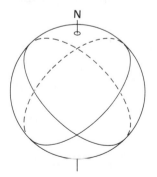
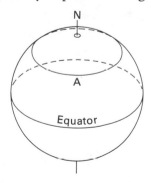

Slicing through a great circle will bisect the globe. *Left:* great circles. *Right:* A is not a great circle.

through the center. The shortest distance between two points on the earth. Long courses, such as across oceans, are plotted as great circles. See **rhumb line.**

Greenwich Mean Time   See **Greenwich Meridian.**

Greenwich Meridian   A great circle through the poles that passes through Greenwich, England, used for measuring longitude and the standard time used in celestial navigation. Formerly **Greenwich Mean Time,** it is now called **Universal Time.** See **geographic coordinates.**

grid   Parallel lines on a chart from which direction can be related.

grog   Originally a mixture of rum and water provided to British sailors. Sometimes refers to any alcoholic drink.

grommet   A reinforcing ring around a hole in a sail. Also, a ring of rope formed by a single strand laid three times around.

ground tackle   General term for anchoring equipment. See **anchor, anchoring.**

gudgeon   See **rudder.**

gunter rig   See **sailing rigs.**

gunwale (pronounced "gunnel")   The upper edge of the side of the hull.

guy   A rope, wire stay, or brace used to steady or guide something. Commonly used in tandem with a spinnaker pole to control a spinnaker's fore-and-aft movement.

gybe   See **jibe.**

h

hail   To call another person or boat. Also, a boat hails from a certain port, or a person from a hometown.

half hitch   See **knots and splices.**

halyard (sometimes **halliard**)   A line used to hoist sails, flags, and some spars.

hand   A crewmember. Also, to take down a sail.

handy-billy   An all-purpose portable tackle generally consisting of a single block and a double block with each sheave on its own pin, called a **fiddle block.** Snapshackles at either end allow quick attachment, and a cam cleat on the fiddle block locks the line. Often used as a boom vang.

hank   Ring, shackle, or piston or snap hook by which a sail is attached to a stay.

hard alee (helm's alee)   Refers to putting the tiller down to leeward or turning the wheel to windward as an announcement that the boat is being tacked. See also **ready about.**

harden   To trim a sheet in more, thus sail closer to the wind.

hatch   An opening in the deck, sometimes with its watertight cover.

haul   To pull on a line.

hawsehole   A hole in the bow through which the anchor cable can be fed. See **hawsepipe.**

hawsepipe   A fitting through a hawsehole that acts as a fairlead for the anchor cable.

hawser (sometimes **hauser**)   See **towline.**

head   Toilet, or the place where the toilet is located. See also **sail parts.**

head off (fall off)   Turn the boat away from the wind. Opposite of **head up.**

head sea   A sea which is traveling in the opposite direction to that of the boat. Opposite of **following sea.**

head up   Turn the boat toward the wind. Opposite of **head off.**

headboard   See **sail parts.**

header   When close-hauled, a windshift forward relative to the boat, requiring the boat to head off.

heading   Direction a boat is pointing.

headsail   A sail set forward of the main mast or foremast.

headstay   See **standing rigging.**

head-to-wind   With the bow facing the wind.

headway   Moving forward. Opposite of **sternway.**

heave   To throw.

heave short   To heave in on the cable until the boat is nearly over her anchor.

heave-to (past tense hove-to)   To slow the boat when on a close reach by backing the headsail and lashing the tiller to leeward. Done by winching the clew to windward, or (dangerous in heavy winds) coming about with the jibsheet kept made fast to the previous leeward cleat, then quickly putting the helm down on the new tack. Also, to slow the boat temporarily when on a beam reach by letting the sails luff.

A sloop hove-to. Wind pressing against jib pushes bow off to port. Boat then develops headway, and rudder takes hold to bring her back up to starboard. Cycle repeats.

heaving line   A light line with a weight on the end, used to throw from a vessel to a dock, or from one vessel to another, so that a heavier dock line or towing line may be hauled across.

heavy weather A combination of strong winds and large seas requiring special steps in order to sail without damage to the vessel or injury to the crew, and ultimately, in order to keep the boat afloat.

heel A boat heels when it lies over at an angle when sailing. Also the bottom end of the mast.

helm The tiller or wheel that controls the rudder.

helm's alee See **hard-a-lee.**

helmsman Person steering.

high aspect ratio See **aspect ratio.**

high and dry A vessel aground, with no water around her.

hike (hike out) When sailing close-hauled on a centerboard boat, to lean out to windward to counteract the heeling of the boat.

hiking strap Fore-and-aft strap attached to the floorboards or centerboard trunk, so that a crewmember can hook his feet and extend his body out to windward to help prevent the boat from heeling excessively.

hitch See **knots and splices.**

hogged Said of a boat whose bow and stern have dropped lower than the midship part of the hull. Opposite of **sagged.**

hoist To raise, such as a sail. Also the length of the luff of a fore-and-aft sail, or the length of the vertical side of an ensign. See **ensign.**

holding ground The quality of the bottom in terms of its ability to hold an anchor.

horizon Place where the sea and sky appear to meet.

horn cleat See **cleat.**

horse See **traveler.**

hounds The place on the mast where lower or intermediate shrouds are secured.

hove-to See **heave-to.**

hug To keep close to, such as a boat sailing close to a shore.

hull The body of a boat, exclusive of her rigging.

hull down When a vessel is so far away that the hull is below the horizon.

hull speed The maximum speed a hull can achieve without planing. For typical hull forms, the square root of the length on the water line times 1.34.

hurricane See **storm warnings.**

hydrometer Instrument used to measure the specific gravity of battery electrolyte, and thus its amount of charge.

impeller (impellor) A small paddlewheel turning on an axle, which, in a power-driven pump, rotates to make the fluid flow, or, in a knotmeter, is rotated by water flowing past the hull to indicate the boat's speed through the water.

This 10-bladed impeller fits over a pump shaft, which goes through the hole in its center.

in irons (in stays) When the boat has stopped or is moving backwards because it is pointing directly into the wind, with sails luffing and no steerageway.

inboard Toward the boat's centerline. Inside the hull. Also an engine permanently installed in a boat, as opposed to mounted on the stern.

Inland Rules See **Rules of the Road.**

inner stay See **standing rigging.**

inshore Toward land. Opposite of **offshore.**

intermediate shrouds See **shrouds.**

International Rules See **Rules of the Road.**

isophase light See **light characteristics.**

jackline (jackstay)   A rigged line to which a safety harness can be clipped. A jackline is also used along the luff of a sail to maintain proper tension.

jacob's ladder   A rope ladder with wooden rungs.

jam cleat   See **cleat.**

jenny   See **genoa.**

jetsam   Anything thrown overboard to lighten the load, and that sinks or is grounded.

jettison   To throw goods overboard.

jetty   A small breakwater. Also a landing or small pier.

jib   The foremost, fore-and-aft, triangular-shaped sail.

jibboom (jib boom)   An extension of the bowsprit.

jibe (gybe)   Swinging over a fore-and-aft sail, to put the stern through the eye of the wind when running before the wind. It may be a controlled jibe or an accidental one.

jib-headed   See **sailing rigs.**

jibsheet   See **running rigging.**

jibstay   See **standing rigging.**

jiffy reefing   See **reefing.**

jigger   The mizzen sail of a ketch or yawl.

jumper stay (jumper)   See **standing rigging.**

jumper struts   See **standing rigging.**

junk   A Chinese sailing vessel.

jury rig   A temporary replacement of any part of the boat's rigging.

kedge To move a vessel by laying out an anchor and hauling on its rode. Kedging off the ground means hauling the vessel back into deep water after she has run aground. A kedge is any small anchor used for kedging. See **anchor.**

keel The fixed underwater part of a sailing boat used to prevent sideways drift and provide stability. Also the main structural member down the boat's centerline, to which the lower ends of the frames are attached.

keelboat A boat with a fixed keel, as opposed to a boat with a centerboard or daggerboard.

keelson (kelson) Structural member fastened to the top of a keel to strengthen it.

keel-stepped Indicates a mast that is stepped on the keel, as opposed to on the deck.

ketch See **sailing rigs.**

king post On a cargo ship, a strong vertical post or column used to support a derrick.

king spoke The spoke on a steering wheel which, when upright, indicates that the rudder is amidships.

knockdown When a boat is laid over on her beam ends by wind or sea, allowing water to come in over the gunwales. After a knockdown a keelboat generally rights itself. A small centerboard boat normally must be righted by the crew. See **capsize.**

knot A measure of speed equal to one nautical mile (6080 feet) per hour. Also see **knots and splices.**

knotmeter An instrument that measures speed through the water and often accumulated mileage by means of a paddlewheel impeller.

knots and splices **Hitches** are generally knots that make fast to objects, while **bends** join two lines. The **running end** of a line is the part used to make the knot, while the **standing part** is the part not used. The **bitter end** is the end of the running end. (It is also the inboard end of an anchor rode.) A **bight** is a bend in a line, while a **loop** is formed by crossing the running end over the standing part. A **turn** is a loop around an object or line. A second loop forms a **round turn.** All hitches and bends are formed by combinations of bights and loops, or turns. Some common usages follow:

  Figure eights and **overhands** are stopper knots, used, for instance, to keep the end of a line from running through a block. **Square knots (reef knots)** are used to tie reef points, or occasionally to join two lines of the same diameter and under constant tension. (A

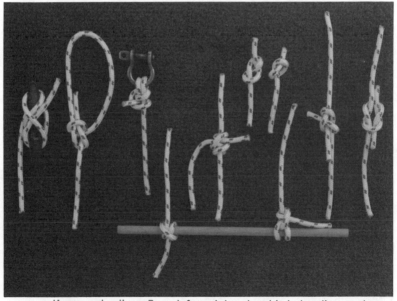

Knots and splices. From left to right: cleat hitch, bowline, anchor bend, clove hitch (on dowel), rolling hitch, figure-eight knot, overhand knot, round turn and two half hitches (on dowel), sheet bend, reef knot.

granny knot is an incorrectly made square knot, which will not hold.) A **sheet bend** joins two lines, particularly of different diameters. When the second half of a sheet bend is applied to a loop or an eye it becomes a **becket hitch.**

A **bowline** forms a temporary loop in the end of a line. A round turn and two **half hitches,** or a **clove hitch** and half hitches make fast to a piling or spar. A **rolling hitch** is used if there will be tension at an angle from the perpendicular of a spar or line, or if the line needs to be loosened quickly. An **anchor bend** (**fisherman's bend**) makes a rode fast to an anchor. A **cleat hitch** makes line fast by a turn, a figure eight across the horns of the cleat, and a half hitch. A **slip knot** is tied for ease in untying by pulling on the running end.

Splices join lines or make permanent loops in their ends by interweaving the strands. A **short splice** is strong, but doubles the diameter, while a **long splice,** although weaker, can be reeved. Wire can be spliced to itself or to rope.

A full coverage of knots and splices important to sailors is presented in *The Essential Knot Book* by Colin Jarman, a volume in the International Marine Seamanship Series.

1

lacing   A line used to secure a sail to its spar.
ladder   Stairs on a boat.
land breeze   Wind blowing from the land out to the sea. Opposite of **sea breeze.**

landfall Arrival at land after an offshore passage. Also sighting land.

landlubber A landsman who knows little about the water.

landmark Any conspicuous object used for piloting.

lanyard A short line used to secure a piece of gear, or to aid in carrying it.

lapper A jib that extends aft of the mast, such as a 110-percent jib. See also **genoa.**

lapstrake (lapstreak) A boat's hull which is made of parallel planks, each of which overlays the outside of the one beneath it, like clapboards on a house.

Lapstrake construction (above), compared to carvel construction (below).

large-scale chart See **chart.**

lash To secure with a line.

lashing A line used to lash.

lateen A triangular fore-and-aft sail on a long yard hoisted on the mast.

lateral resistance Resistance to the leeward or sideways movement of a boat caused by wind or wave forces. Determined by the amount of heel, and by the keel or centerboard below the waterline. See **center of lateral resistance.**

latitude See **geographic coordinates.**

lay Direction of rope twist, usually from right to left.

lay up To store a boat during the winter. Also, to put a boat out of commission.

Right-hand lay. The end of this nylon rope was fused with a soldering iron to prevent fraying.

lazarette   Compartment for gear stowage, often in the stern of a boat.

lazy   Describes any line or gear that does not move or is not used often.

lazy guy   A guy that is not in use, or is taking no strain.

lazyjacks   Lines extending from the mast to the boom that catch, channel, and hold a sail when it is lowered.

leach   See **leech**.

lead   (If pronounced "led"): A lead weight attached to the end of a line, used to determine water depth and the nature of the bottom. (If pronounced "leed"): The path taken by a line, usually between a sail and a fairlead or winch.

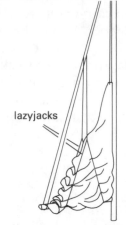

lazyjacks

lead line   Line secured to the lead used for soundings. Generally marked for depths.

lee   The downwind side. To be in the lee of an object is to be sheltered by it.

lee cloth   A cloth fitted to the inboard side of a bunk to prevent the occupant from falling out. See also **leeboard**.

lee helm   Said of a sailboat that falls off the wind to leeward when the helm is free. Generally indicates a dangerously unbalanced sail trim. See **center of effort**.

Lead line

lee shore   The land to leeward of a boat. Opposite of **weather shore**.

leeboard A pivoting board fixed to the outside of the hull to prevent leeway. Also a board fitted to the inboard side of a bunk to prevent the occupant from falling out. See **lee cloth.**

leech See **sail parts.**

leech cord See **sail parts.**

leech line See **sail parts.**

leeward (pronounced "loo-ard") The direction away from the wind. Opposite of **windward.**

leeway Sideways motion of the boat to leeward, caused by the wind.

length at waterline (LWL) The designed length of the waterline when the boat floats upright in the water. See **hull speed.**

lie off To keep a little distance from shore or another boat.

lie-to A sailboat lies-to with her head to the wind by setting a mizzen or riding sail and lashing the helm amidships. Also describes a boat underway with no way on, or one that is hove-to. See **heave-to.**

life buoy (life ring) A ring, or U-shaped buoy, to support a person in the water.

life jacket See **PFD.**

life raft A raft for emergency use in case of sinking, generally inflatable if for use in sailboats.

lifeline Safety line fitted around an open deck.

lift (lifter) A windshift farther aft relative to the boat, allowing the boat to head up when sailing close-hauled. Also short for **topping lift.**

light and buoy list See **light characteristics.**

light beacon See **beacon.**

light characteristics Buoys and beacons are identified at night by their colors and the relative times they are on or extinguished. A **fixed light** is continuous. A **flashing light** is off more than it is on. An **equal interval** (or **isophase**) **light** is on the same amount of time it is off. An **occulting light** is on more than it is off. Numerous multiple combinations of these basic characteristics exist. They are set out on individual NOAA charts and explained in the *Light and Buoy List,* published annually by the U.S. Government Printing Office.

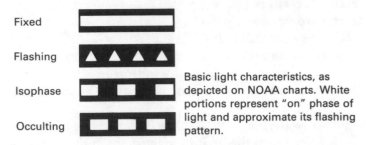

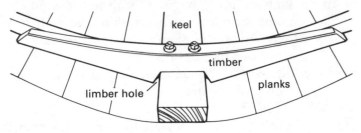

Basic light characteristics, as depicted on NOAA charts. White portions represent "on" phase of light and approximate its flashing pattern.

limber holes   Gaps at the lower end of frames, above the keel, to allow water to drain to the lowest point of the bilges.

line   A rope chosen for a specific function on a boat.

line of position (LOP)   In navigation, an imaginary line somewhere along which the boat lies. It can be calculated from the reciprocal of a bearing taken on a recognized object, from a radio direction finder reading, from a range, from a line of equal water depths (contour navigation), or through celestial navigation calculations.

list   A vessel lists, or has a list, when it inclines to port or starboard due to improper trim or shifted cargo.

lock   The part of a canal or waterway between two floodgates, by means of which a vessel is transferred from a higher to a lower level or vice versa.

locker   A storage compartment.

log A book or journal in which are recorded principal events which have occurred while on board, such as distances covered, course sailed, and weather conditions. Also the act of recording in a log. Also an instrument used to measure the boat's speed through the water or distance traveled through the water. See **speed log.**

TIME	COURSE Comp. Dev. Var. True	LOG Read. Dist.	WIND Dir. Force	BARO.	POSITION Lat. Long.	NOTES
1130					30.26 25°57.8'N 81°43.78'	Underway for Key West
1215	186		010 3-4	30.20	CP RHW (M0A)	Smith Shoal 75.1 M
1400	–	6.4	– –	30.18	25°52.65 81°47.07	" " 68.7"
1600	–	9.0 15.4	– 4	30.15	25°42.80 81°46.49	" " 59.7"
1800	–	8.1 23.5	070 2-3	–	25°34.06 81°44.08	" " 51.6"
2000	181	7.7 31.2	– –	–	25°26.20 81°43.31	" " 43.9"
2200	–	7.7 38.9	– –	–	25°18.52 81°45.43	" " 36.2
2400	200	8.0 46.9	160 2-3	–	25°10.95 81°48.39	" " 28.2
12/23 0200	187	– –	– –	–	24°57.04 81°50.68	– – –
0400	190	14.7 61.6	010 –	30.10	24°56.82 81°54.12	" " 13.5
0730	INBOUND	– 75.1	010 2-3	30.10	Smith Shoal	Inbound for Key West
1130	–	– –	– –	–	Key West Yacht Club	– Docked

MARCO ISLAND – KEY WEST
Day's Run   Average Speed   Fuel **18**   Consumed **2.5** Received **2.5** Remaining **18**
Engine Log: Beginning **323.50** End **338.75** Hours Used **15.25**
Signature: *Fred Edwards, Captain*

LOG

Typical entry in the ship's log for *Semper Fi,* the author's sloop.

long splice See **knots and splices.**

longitude See **geographic coordinates.**

loom The glow of a light that is below the horizon, or of a form partially obscured by fog.

loop See **knots and splices.**

loose To loose a sail is to unfurl it.

loose-footed sail A sail that is secured to the boom at the tack and clew only, as opposed to a sail whose foot is laced to the boom or secured with slides.

Loran-C   Acronym for LOng RAnge Navigation. An extremely sophisticated automatic navigation system that makes possible precise and reliable position fixes. The Loran-C system consists of groups of radio transmitters that broadcast synchronized, pulsed signals. Shipboard receivers measure the precise time difference between the reception of signals from two stations; this information is then converted, either automatically by the receiver or with the aid of a Loran-C overprinted chart, to establish a position. Explanation and use of Loran-C is covered in *Piloting with Electronics* by Luke Melton, a volume in the International Marine Seamanship Series.

LOP   See **line of position.**

low aspect ratio   See **aspect ratio.**

low water   The lowest level reached by each tide.

lower shrouds   See **standing rigging.**

lubber line   See **compass.**

luff   To bring the boat's head closer to the wind. To **luff up** is to turn its head into the wind. A sail luffs when it is into the wind and flapping. See **slat.** See also **sail parts.**

luff up   See **luff.**

luff woolly   See **telltale.**

lug (lugsail)   See **sailing rigs.**

LWL   See **length at waterline.**

magnetic north   The point to which the north-seeking pole of a magnetic compass is drawn.

magnetic variation   See **compass.**

main   The principal object of several similar ones, such as mainmast, main deck, mainsail, etc. Also short for mainsail.

mainsheet   See **running rigging.**

make fast   To secure a line, generally to a cleat or to bitts.

make water   To take on water from a leak or flooding. Also, a raw-water-cooled engine makes water through its exhaust.

marconi rig   See **sailing rigs.**

mark   An object that is a guide when navigating or a turning point when racing.

marlinespike (marlinspike, fid)   A pointed tapering spike used for opening the strands of rope when splicing.

marlinespike seamanship   The art of using ropes, lines, knots, splices, blocks, and tackle.

martingale   See **bobstay.**

mast   A spar set upright to support rigging and sails.

mast coat   Waterproof skirt lashed or taped tightly around a mast, with its lower edge secured to a collar to make the joint between deck and mast watertight. See also **collar.**

mast hole   The place where the mast passes through the deck of a keel-stepped boat.

mast partners   Structure to reinforce the opening where a mast goes through a deck or cabinhouse.

mast step   A shaped brace on which, or into which, the foot of a mast rests.

masthead   The top of the mast.

masthead light   See **navigation lights.**

masthead rig (masthead sloop)   See **standing rigging.**

mate (also first mate)   The captain's senior assistant.

mean high tide   See **tide.**

mean low tide   See **tide.**

Mediterranean moor   See **anchoring.**

mercator projection   See **chart.**

meridian   A great circle at right angles to the equator and passing through the poles. Lines of longitude are meridians.

messenger   A lightweight line used to haul a heavier line.

midship (midships)   The midship spoke is the upper spoke of the wheel when the rudder is lined up fore-and-aft. See also **amidships**.

mile   See **nautical mile**.

millibar   A unit of barometric pressure.

miss stays   A boat misses stays when in tacking it fails to go about.

mizzen   The after and smaller mast of a ketch or yawl. Also a sail set on that mast.

mole   A massive work formed of masonry and large stones or earth laid in the sea as a pier or breakwater. Also the harbor formed by such a structure.

monkey fist (monkey's fist)   A knot worked into the end of a heaving line enclosing a weight, so that the line will carry when thrown.

moor   To make a vessel fast with cables, lines, or anchors.

mooring   A place where, or an object to which, a vessel can be made fast.

mooring buoy   A buoy which is anchored permanently, to which a vessel can be moored.

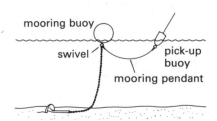

mooring pendant   A line used to secure a boat to a mooring buoy, which is in turn permanently attached to the anchor.

motorsailer A combination sail-and-powerboat, generally heavier than a sailboat and with larger accommodations.

mouse To put turns of small stuff (light cordage, yard, or line) around the end of a hook or hank and its standing part when it is hooked to anything, to prevent its slipping out.

nameboard Board attached to the hull, usually at the stern, on which a boat's name is painted or carved.

narrows Any small passage or channel between land.

nautical almanac An annual publication containing astronomical and tidal information for sailors and navigators.

nautical mile One minute of latitude, approximately 6080 feet, or 1/8 longer than the statute mile of 5280 feet.

navigation The art and science of finding the position of a boat and of conducting a boat safely from one point to another.

navigation lights (running lights) Lights required to be shown at night, to enable identification of a vessel's size, direction of movement, and special characteristics affecting maneuverability. Basic lights include **sidelights** (red to port and green to starboard); a **masthead light** in white, and a white or amber **sternlight**.

On larger vessels white masthead lights on separate masts (the after light carried at least 2 meters higher than the forward one) serve as **range lights,** which identify the angle on the bow to determine if danger of collision exists.

A detailed explanation of navigation light combinations is presented in *Sailing at Night* by Richard Henderson, a volume in the International Marine Seamanship Series.

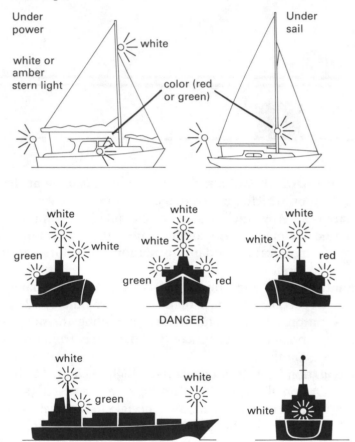

navigator's balls   See **quadrantal correctors.**
neap tide   See **tide.**
Neptune   Mythical god of the sea.

nest or nested Naval equivalent of **rafting up**. Also a small boat stowed inside another.

nettle A short line for lashing a small object.

no-go zone Area so close to the eye of the wind that the boat cannot sail into it.

nominal range The range of a light in 10 miles' visibility, governed solely by the power of the light, and not taking into account the height of the light or the observer, or the curvature of the earth.

not under command Said of a vessel unable to maneuver, usually due to a mechanical malfunction.

nun buoy See **buoy.**

oakum A caulking material for wooden boats, generally made of tarred hemp rope fiber.

oar An implement for rowing and sometimes steering a boat.

oarlocks (rowlocks) Devices that secure oars to a boat or dinghy to form a fulcrum for rowing.

observed position A boat's position as plotted on a chart through the identification of landmarks or aids to navigation.

occulting light See **light characteristics.**

off the wind Sailing to leeward (in the same direction as the wind) with the sheets eased (slacked off). Opposite of **on the wind.**

offshore Away from the shore.

oil canning Hull flex in unsupported sections of a fiberglass boat underway. Makes a popping noise similar to that made when squirting oil from a can.

oilskins (skins) Old term sometimes used for modern foul-weather clothing.

on her beam ends See **beam ends.**

on the beach See **beach.**

on the bottom See **aground.**

on the quarter See **quarter.**

on the wind Close-hauled. Opposite of **off the wind.**

one-design A boat built to conform to rules so that it is identical to all others in the same racing class.

onshore Toward the shore. An **onshore breeze** blows from the sea toward the land.

outboard Toward or beyond the boat's sides. Also a detachable motor mounted on the stern of a boat.

outfoot To sail faster than another boat when sailing close-hauled.

outhaul A line, or block and tackle, that hauls out something, such as the mainsail outhaul that hauls the clew of the mainsail out to the after end of the boom. See **running rigging.**

outpoint To sail closer to the wind than another boat.

overboard Over the side, or out of the boat.

overhand See **knots and splices.**

overhang The projection of the stern beyond the sternpost, or the bow beyond the stem.

overhaul To pull out slack in the parts of a sheet or tackle so as to slack it when it is not under strain. Also, to overtake another boat.

overhead Same as the ceiling in a house.

overpowered Carrying too much sail for the wind strength.

packing gland   See **stuffing box.**

paddle   A small oar used to propel a boat from the side or stern without oarlocks.

padeye   A U-shaped fitting with both legs permanently secured to the deck or a spar, used as a catch for rigging, hooks, etc.

painter   A line attached to the bow of a small boat, used for towing or making her fast.

This dinghy is made fast by her painter.

palm   A leather band, with a reinforced center, which is strapped to the palm of the hand and assists in pushing a needle through heavy material.

parallel rulers (parallel rules)   Two rulers joined so that they remain parallel when moved apart. Used to transfer courses and bearings to a chart's compass rose, or to transfer com-

Parallel rulers

pass or true readings from the rose to another location on the chart.

part   A line parts when it breaks. See also **carry away.** Also, the unit of ropes in a tackle, sheet, or dockline, such as a three-part sheet.

partners   See **mast partners.**

passageway   Corridor or hallway in a vessel.

patent log   See **speed logs.**

pay off   When sailing, to fall away from the wind.

pay out   To ease out a line, or allow it to run in a controlled manner.

peak   The upper outer corner of a four-sided sail, usually applied to a gaff sail. Also the upper end of a gaff.

peak halyards   The lines hoisting the peak of a quadrilateral sail.

pelican hook   A hinged hook held closed by a ring.

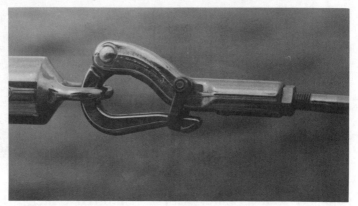

Pelican hook

pelorus   An instrument for taking bearings relative to the fore-and-aft line of the boat. May be mounted on a compass to take compass bearings.

pendant (pronounced "pennant")   Any short extension rope or wire added, for example, to a tack or clew. Also the line by which a boat is made fast to a mooring buoy.

pennant   A tapered flag.

period   See **seas.**

PFD (personal flotation device)   Cushion or life jacket used to keep a person afloat.

pier   A structure extending into the water for use as a landing place. See also **dock, quay, wharf.**

pig stick   The staff used to fly a burgee from the masthead.

pile (piling)   An upright pole driven into the bottom and projecting above the surface of the water, to which a craft may be made fast.

pilot   A person licensed, or otherwise qualified, to advise the captain how to navigate the vessel through congested and/or dangerous waters, particularly into or out of harbors and rivers.

piloting   Navigation by use of visible references, such as landmarks, aids to navigation, depth of water, etc.

pinch   To sail a boat so close to the wind that the sails begin to stall.

pintle   See **rudder.**

piston hook   A type of snaphook in which the hook opening is closed and opened by a spring-loaded piston.

pitch   A boat's motion around a horizontal, athwartships axis. Also the amount of twist in a propeller blade.

pitchpole   A boat pitchpoles when it is thrown stern-over-bow by a wave from astern.

pivot point   Point in a boat about which she turns.

plane   To gain hydrodynamic lift, allowing much higher speed.

planing hull   A type of hull shaped to begin planing at high-speed. See **displacement hull.**

planking   The boards used to cover the frames of a hull. See also **carvel** and **lapstrake.**

plot   To lay out courses, bearings, and directions on a chart. A plot is the result.

point   To sail close to the wind, or the ability to do so. Also one of 32 points of the compass, each of which equals 11¹/₄ degrees. Also a geographical projection from a coastline.

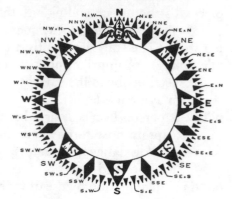

Converting compass points to degrees and vice versa. (See table on opposite page.)

point high   To sail very close to the wind.

points of sailing (points of sail)   The angles relative to the wind on which a boat may sail.

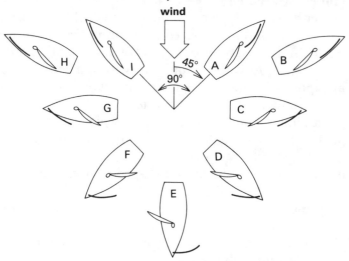

Points of sailing: A) close-hauled; B) close reach; C) beam reach; D) broad reach; E) run (wing-and-wing); F) broad reach; G) beam reach; H) close reach; I) close-hauled. Boats A through D are on the port tack; F through I are on the starboard tack.

Points	Degrees
North (N)	0 00'
North by East (N x E)	11 15'
North Northeast (NNE)	22 30'
Northeast by North (NE x N)	33 45'
Northeast (NE)	45 00'
Northeast by East (NE x E)	56 15'
East Northeast (ENE)	67 30'
East by North (E x N)	78 45'
East (E)	90 00'
East by South (E x S)	101 15'
East Southeast (ESE)	112 30'
Southeast by East (SE x E)	123 45'
Southeast (SE)	135 00'
Southeast by South (SE x S)	146 15'
South Southeast (SSE)	157 30'
South by East (S x E)	168 45'
South (S)	180 00'
South by West (S x W)	191 15'
South Southwest (SSW)	202 30'
Southwest by South (SW x S)	213 45'
Southwest (SW)	225 00'
Southwest by West (SW x W)	236 15'
West Southwest (WSW)	247 30'
West by South (W x S)	258 45'
West (W)	270 00'
West by North (W x N)	281 15'
West Northwest (WNW)	292 30'
Northwest by West (NW x W)	303 45'
Northwest (NW)	315 00'
Northwest by North (NW x N)	326 15'
North Northwest (NNW)	337 30'
North by West (N x W)	348 45'
North (N)	360 00'

poop   A raised stern deck. A boat is pooped when a wave comes over the stern.

port   The left side of a boat when facing the bow. Also a harbor or harbor town. See also **portlight**.

portlight (porthole)   A window set into a reinforcing frame in a boat. Often called a porthole, or port, if it is designed to let in fresh air.

port tack   See **tack**.

preventer   A line or tackle set up to prevent movement of a mast or boom. A **boom preventer** is a line, tackle, or boom vang rigged to prevent an accidental jibe.

privileged vessel   See **stand-on vessel**.

prop walk   Sideways effect of the propeller on the stern of a boat, particularly at slow speeds.

propeller (propellor, screw)   A device containing slanted (pitched) blades that fits on a shaft coupled to the engine and moves the boat when under power.

protest signal   A signal (a red flag) that is hoisted during a sailing race when the skipper believes the boat has been fouled by another competitor.

protractor   An instrument showing the degree divisions of a half circle, used in plotting angles.

provisions   Stores, food.

prow   The bow and fore part of a vessel above the water-line.

psychrometer   See **sling psychrometer**.

pucker string   See **sail parts**.

puff   A gust of wind.

pulley   See **block**.

pulpit   An elevated guardrail set up at either the bow or the stern or both. The one at the stern is sometimes called a **stern rail, taffrail,** or **pushpit**.

punt   Flat-bottomed boat, square at either end, usually propelled by a pole. Suitable for shallow, protected waters.

purchase   Any tackle or system of leverage used to raise or move an object. To get a purchase on the object is to create such leverage.

q

quadrantal correctors or spheres (navigator's balls)   Two iron balls, secured at either side of the binnacle, which, by movement toward or away from the compass, help compensate for magnetic deviation.

quarantine flag (Q-flag)   A rectangular yellow flag flown upon entering a foreign port until the boat has been formally cleared by immigration authorities.

quarter   The after part of a boat on each side of the stern. Every boat thus has a starboard and a port quarter. **On the quarter** means a bearing 45 degrees off the stern.

quarter berth   A bunk in the cabin, located underneath one side of the cockpit.

quarter bitts   See **bitts.**

quarter wave   See **stern wave.**

quartering   Steering so as to keep the wind or waves on the quarter.

quartering sea   Sea coming on a boat's quarter.

quay   A man-made stone or concrete bank in the water used for a landing place to load and unload cargo and passengers. Pronounced "key" but sometimes "kway."

race A strong confused current, generally caused by a confluence of currents.

radar An electronic instrument for detecting and locating vessels, floating objects, and terrain configurations during periods of low visibility or at distances beyond the range of eyesight. Description and usage of radar is given in *Piloting with Electronics* by Luke Melton, a volume in the International Marine Seamanship Series.

radio beacon See **beacon.**

radio direction finder Apparatus for taking bearings on the source of radio transmissions.

raft up To secure one or more boats alongside another, using lines. See **nest.**

rail Uppermost edge of a bulwark, or upper and outer edge of the hull of a craft having no bulwark.

raise To perceive a vessel or object when it rises above the horizon or otherwise comes within visible distance. Also, to get someone to respond on the radio.

rake The angle of a mast from the perpendicular, usually aft.

ram's horn See **reefing.**

range A pair of landmarks or navigational aids, which, when aligned one behind the other, will place the boat on a line of position or indicate when it is within a channel. See also **tide.**

This photo was taken while putting front range close aboard to starboard. From a distance (where ranges are needed), front range will be seen below back range; if directly below, boat is safely aligned.

range lights   See **navigation lights.**

rating   A method of measuring certain dimensions of yachts of different sizes and forms so that they can race on a handicap basis.

ratlines (pronounced "ratlins")   Small lines or rods tied horizontally across the shrouds to form steps, used for climbing the mast or for better observation.

Ratlines

reach   Any point of sailing between close-hauled and running, that is, with the wind more than 45 degrees off the bow, but less than 180. Subdivided into **close** (wind forward of the beam), **beam,** and **broad** (wind aft of the beam) **reach.**

ready about   An order to stand by in preparation for coming about. When the crew and boat are ready, the command is followed by "hard alee" or "helm's alee." See **hard alee.**

reciprocal bearing   When taking a bearing on an object, the reciprocal is the bearing from the object to the observer, obtained by subtracting 180 degrees from the bearing, if possible, or otherwise adding 180 degrees. The reciprocal becomes a line of position.

reef   Sand, coral, or other natural obstructions in shallow water. Also see **reefing.**

reef band   See **reefing.**

reef cringles   See **reefing.**

reef knot   See **knots and splices.**

reef points   See **reefing.**

reefing   Reducing the area of a sail. A mainsail is **roller reefed** by rotating the boom or mast, which rolls the sail around it.

A mainsail is **jiffy reefed** (also called **slab reefed**) by partly lowering the sail. Leech and luff earings, passed through **reef cringles** (thimbles, rings, or grommets), may be used to secure the partially lowered sail at the leech and luff respectively; or the luff cringle may be brought directly to a hook, which if curved concentrically is called a **ram's horn.** Excess material at the foot of the reduced sail (known as the **bunt**) is secured by furling lines—either a single lacing line, or several short pieces of line (**nettles**). If sewn to the sail, these furling lines and their points of attachment are often called **reef points.** The furling lines can also hang on each side of the sail from grommets set in horizontal reinforcing materials (**reef bands**) sewn into the sail.

Headsails, foresails, staysails, and mizzens can also be rigged for jiffy reefing.

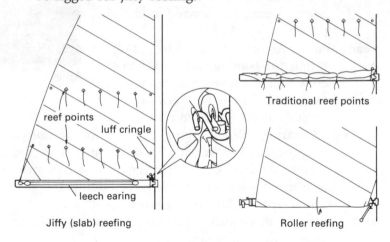

reef points

luff cringle

Traditional reef points

leech earing

Jiffy (slab) reefing   Roller reefing

reeve (past tense rove)   To pass a line through a block or other fitting.

relative bearing   Direction of an object measured in relation to the bow of the boat, which is designated 000 degrees.

relative wind   See **wind.**

rhumb line   A course that crosses all meridians at the same angle. It shows as a straight line on mercator projections, and is essentially accurate for distances less than 1,000 miles. See **great circle.**

ribs   See **frames.**

ride   To lie at anchor. Also, to ride out a gale is to heave-to and wait for a gale to pass when at sea.

riding light   An all-around white light shown while riding at anchor, usually hoisted on the forestay.

riding sail   A small sail set to a backstay or topping lift used to keep the boat head-to-wind when anchored or hove-to.

riding weight   See **anchoring.**

rig   The arrangement of a boat's mast, spars, and sails. To rig a boat is to set up her spars and standing and running rigging. See also **sailing rigs.**

rigging   The general term for the wire and rope lines used to secure masts and sails. See **running rigging, standing rigging.**

rip   See **tide rip.**

rise   See **tide.**

roach   See **sail parts.**

roadstead   An anchorage for ships, at a distance from shore, and generally unprotected.

rode   See **anchor** and **anchoring.**

roll   A boat's motion around a horizontal, fore-and-aft axis.

roller furling   Type of jib or mainsail rigged to furl by rolling up around its own luff.

Roller furling system using an extrusion fitted around the forestay. When a headsail is fitted into a slide of the extrusion and hoisted, the extrusion can be revolved (using line attached to the drum), thus rolling (furling) the sail around it, similar to the action of a window shade. (Courtesy of Cruising Design, Inc.)

roller reefing   See **reefing.**

rolling hitch   See **knots and splices.**

rope   Cordage as it is purchased at the store. When it is put to use aboard a boat, it generally becomes **line.**

rote   The noise of surf on shore.

round up   A boat rounds up when its bow moves up to weather.

round turn   See **knots and splices.**

rove   See **reeve.**

rowlocks   See **oarlocks.**

rubbing strake   A wood beading serving as a rubrail.

rubrail   A structural member running around the outside of the boat near the gunwale to protect the hull from damage when touching piers or other boats.

rudder   A flat surface hung from the boat vertically into the water, which changes the boat's heading when pivoted by a tiller or wheel. It can be transom-hung by inserting **pintles** (pins) into gudgeons (eyes), or it can be mounted on a sternpost. It can also be shaft-mounted

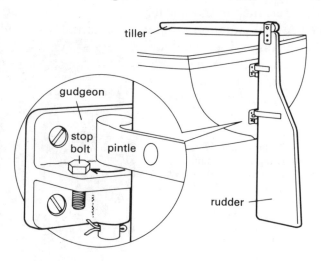

This rudder is transom-hung, using pintles and gudgeons.

using a **rudder post** (also known as a **rudder stock**.) If shaft-mounted, the rudder post goes through a bearing tube that is normally sealed at the bottom by a **stuffing box**. A shaft-mounted rudder may be attached to a skeg (a continuation of the keel aft) under the hull, or it may be a **spade** (free-hung) **rudder.**

Rudder shaft-mounted on a partial skeg.

Rules of the Road Navigational safety regulations governing identification and movement of vessels in relation to each other. **Inland Rules** are enacted by Congress for the inland waters of the United States. **International Rules** (called 1972 International Regulations for Preventing Collisions at Sea, or **COLREGS** for short) are established by agreement among maritime nations for vessels in international waters.

run To sail with the wind aft, or very nearly so. Also to allow a line to feed freely.

running backstay See **standing rigging.**

running end See **knots and splices.**

running fix A fix obtained by advancing a line of position (LOP) taken from a recognized object so that it crosses a later LOP taken from the same object. See **line of position, dead reckoning.**

running free Sailing with the wind on the quarter, i.e., on a broad reach.

running lights   See **navigation lights.**

running rigging   All wire and lines that are hauled on when handling sails. A **halyard,** identified by the sail it serves, is used to hoist a sail. A **sheet,** identified by the sail it serves, is used to trim the sail or adjust its angle in relation to wind direction, and when on the wind to exert downward pull on the leech to preserve shape. **Jibsheets** generally come in pairs (one sheet on each side of the boat), and are led to winches by fairleads and sheet blocks. **Mainsheets,** (and sheets for other boomed sails on a twin-masted boat) are often rove through travelers that move from side to side on deck horses or bridles to adjust the sail shape relative to the wind. A **topping lift** supports the weight of the boom when the sail is lowered. A **clew outhaul** controls the tension of the foot of a sail. A **downhaul** is a tackle

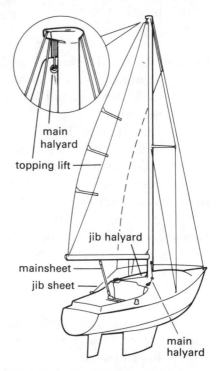

main
halyard

topping lift

jib halyard

mainsheet

jib sheet

main
halyard

Running rigging

attached to the gooseneck of a fore-and-aft sail to adjust the tension of the luff. A downhaul is also a line led
from the head of a headsail and through a block at the
foot of the stay for hauling down the sail.

S

safety harness A harness with a line and shackle, used to
attach crew to a boat in heavy weather, at night, or
when singlehanding.

sagged Said of a boat whose midship part of the hull has
dropped lower than bow and stern. The opposite of
hogged.

sail Vertical airfoil that uses wind pressure to propel a boat.
Can be made of cloth, plastics, wood, metal, etc.

sail measurements For developing or determining a boat's
sail plan, the following terms apply: I = foretriangle
height, J = fore-
triangle base, P =
mainsail luff, E =
mainsail foot. The
accompanying il-
lustration shows
how these terms
are applied. See
also **genoa.**

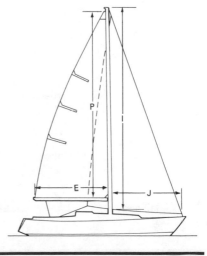

Sail measurements

sail parts   On a triangular fore-and-aft sail the **luff** is the forward edge, the **leech** is the after edge, and the **foot** is the bottom edge; the **head** is the top corner, the **tack** is the forward lower corner, and the **clew** is the after lower corner.

Tabling is folded-over reinforcing material sewn along the corners and edges. A **headboard** is a plastic or metal reinforcement at the head. A **roach** is a convex curve at the leech. **Battens** are thin strips of wood or plastic inserted in pockets in the roach to support it in light airs. A **leech cord** (also **pucker string**) leads from head to clew and adjusts to eliminate leech flutter, and to give it more curve in light winds.

A **squaresail** has a leech at either side. The **head** of a gaff sail is the upper edge. The **throat** is the forward upper corner, and the **peak** is the after upper corner. See **reefing.**

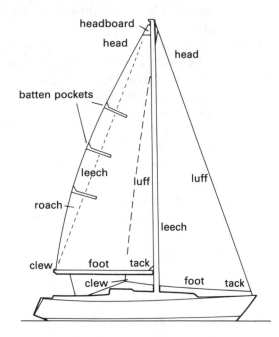

Sail parts

sail stops   Short lengths of line used to wrap around a sail when it is bundled up or furled. Also called **furling lines, gaskets.**

sailing free   See **running free.**

sailing rigs   The pattern of spars and sails on a vessel, designed for speed or ease of handling, or some combination thereof. The most common types of rigs are:

bark   A three- (or more) masted, square-rigged vessel with fore-and-aft sails on the after mast.

barkentine   A bark with only the foremast square-rigged.

brig   A two-masted, square-rigged vessel.

brigantine   A brig with a fore-and-aft main.

catboat   A boat with the mainsail attached to a mast stepped well forward and no headsail.

cutter   A single-masted boat with the mast stepped from 40 percent to 50 percent of the deck length aft of the bow,

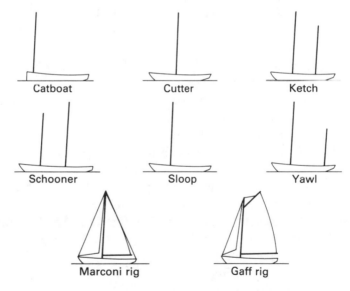

Common fore-and-aft sailing rigs

allowing for a mainsail and two headsails—an inner staysail and an outer jib.

gaff rig A four-sided, fore-and-aft sail with the head extended by a gaff.

gunter rig A fore-and-aft rig with a club that slides up the mast to form an extension of the mast.

ketch A two-masted, fore-and-aft rigged boat. The forward mast is the mainmast. The mizzenmast, which is smaller, is stepped aft of the mainmast and forward of the rudder post.

lug (lugsail) A fore-and-aft, four-sided sail bent onto a yard that extends part of the sail forward of the mast.

marconi rig (jib-headed, Bermudian) A tall, triangular, fore-and-aft sail, as distinguished from a gaff rig.

schooner A two-masted fore-and-aft rigged vessel whose mainmast is the after mast. Big schooners may have three or more masts.

sloop A single-masted, fore-and-aft rigged boat whose working sails are main and jib. It can be gaff- or marconi-rigged.

square rig A method of rigging four-sided sails so that they hang athwartships.

yawl A two-masted, fore-and-aft rigged boat similar to a ketch except that the mizzenmast is smaller and is stepped aft of the rudder post.

saloon (salon) The main cabin, or that part of the cabin that contains a dining or relaxation area.

samson post A strong vertical post or bitt onto which lines or rodes can be secured.

satnav Acronyn for SATellite NAVigation. An electronic navigational system that converts satellite signals to fixes.

schooner See **sailing rigs**.

scope See **anchoring**.

screw See **propeller**.

scudding See **bare poles**.

sculling Moving an oar back and forth in a figure-eight motion at the stern to propel a boat. Also, in a less strict sense, moving a tiller back and forth to propel the boat.

scuppers Drains for the weather decks or cockpit.

sea anchor Device (often a canvas cone) to stream from the boat, which by its drag helps keep the bow into the wind and sea. Does not touch bottom. See also **drogue.**

sea breeze An onshore midday or afternoon breeze caused by warm air rising over the land and air over the water flowing in to fill the void. Opposite of a **land breeze.**

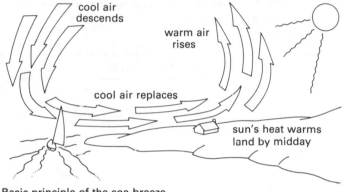

Basic principle of the sea breeze

sea room A safe maneuvering distance from the shore or other hazards.

sea state See **seas.**

seacock See **through-hull fitting.**

seas The combination of swells (swell waves) from afar and locally generated wind waves. **Wave length** is measured from one crest (top) to the next. As wave length decreases, waves become choppy. **Wave height** is the distance from the **trough** (bottom) to the crest. **Speed** is the velocity of a crest (although the water moves little). **Period** is the time the wave takes to pass a given point. **Breaking seas** have crests that spill or fall into the troughs. **Sea state** is the height of the seas and is described in a numerical table.

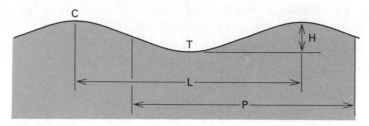

Wave characteristics: L = length, H = height, C = crest, T = trough, P = period (the time in seconds the wave takes to pass a given point).

Sea State Table

Description and wave heights	Sea state	Description and waves heights	Sea state
Calm glassy 0	0	Rough 8 to 13 feet	5
Rippled 0 to 1 foot	1	Very rough 13 to 20 feet	6
Smooth 1 to 2 feet	2	High 20 to 30 feet	7
Slight 2 to 4 feet	3	Very high 30 to 45 feet	8
Moderate 4 to 8 feet	4	Phenomenal over 45 feet	9

seaworthy A boat or its gear if in fit condition to meet the sea.
secure To make fast. Also, to properly stow loose gear.
seize To fasten lines together by turns of small stuff. See **small stuff.**

self-steering A steering system which when set maintains a boat on a constant course relative to the wind. Usually employs a mechanical wind vane system.

wind vane

Wind vane in a self-steering system.

set To set a sail is to hoist it so that it may be used for propulsion. See also **tidal current.**

set flying A sail made fast only at its corners, such as a spinnaker.

seven-eighths rig See **standing rigging.**

sextant An instrument used for measuring angles accurately. See **celestial navigation.**

Sextant

shackle A U-shaped connector with a pin or bolt across the open end. A **snapshackle** is a hook with a spring-loaded safety catch across the open end, often used in the quantities needed to attach sail to a stay.

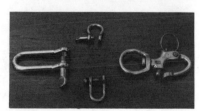

Shackles

shake To cast off or loosen, as in shaking out a reef.

shaft A rod coupled to an inboard engine's transmission, and leading through a stuffing box in the hull, then through a cutlass bearing embedded in an external strut, to the end of which is attached the propeller.

The shaft goes through a cutlass bearing located in the strut. Propeller will be locked on by a key placed in the slot at the left end and secured with a nut and cotter pin. Zinc fits around the shaft at the right of the strut.

shank See **anchor.**

sheave (**pronounced "shiv"**) The grooved wheel in a block.

sheer The upper edge of a boat's hull; especially, the curve or sweep in profile of this upper edge.

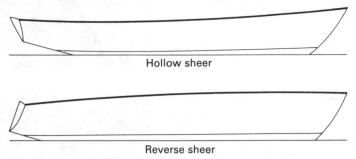

Hollow sheer

Reverse sheer

sheet See **running rigging.**

sheet bend See **knots and splices.**

sheet block A block that makes up part of the tackle on a sheet or leads a sheet to its cleat or winch. See **running rigging.**

shell   The casing of a block that holds the pin.

ship   An ocean-going vessel, generally large enough to carry a boat on board. A boat ships a sea when a large wave breaks over it.

shock cord   Strong elasticized rope.

short splice   See **knots and splices.**

short stay   The condition of an anchor rode that has very little scope.

shorten sail   To take in or reef some of the sails.

shrouds   See **standing rigging.**

sidelights   See **navigation lights.**

single up   To reduce all docklines to one point, preparatory to getting underway.

singlehanding   To sail alone, without a crew.

skeg   A continuation of the keel aft, protecting the propeller, from which might be hung the rudder.

skipper   See **captain.**

slab reefing   See **reefing.**

slack   Not fastened, loose. Also to loosen, ease, or let out a line.

slack tide or **slack water**   See **tidal current.**

slat   Sails slat when there is not enough wind to keep them from slapping due to wave action.

slides   Hardware used to attach the foot and/or luff of a sail to a track on a boom or mast respectively.

sling psychrometer   An instrument used to determine the spread between air temperature and dew point. As the spread nears zero, fog occurs.

slip   A berth or location at a dock where a boat may be made fast on both sides.

slip knot   See **knots and splices.**

slip line   A doubled line with both ends made fast on board.

sloop   See **sailing rigs.**

slot effect   The slot is the opening between the mainsail and the jib through which the wind is funneled. The funneling action increases the speed of the air flowing past the leeward side of the main. Following Bernoulli's Principle, the faster flowing air creates less pressure, thus causing suction on the lee side (more pressure on the windward) and increasing the efficiency of the main. The result of the slot effect is to make a main and jib combination more effective than the sum of each alone.

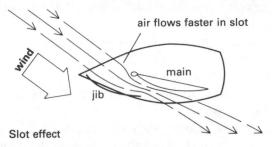

Slot effect

small craft advisory   See **storm warnings.**
small stuff   Light cordage, yarn, or line.
snapshackle (snaphook)   See **shackle.**
small-scale chart   See **chart.**
snatch block   A block into which a line can be placed from the side without having to be reeved.
snotter   A becket for receiving the lower end of a sprit.
snub   To check or brake a line by taking a turn around a bitt, cleat, or winch, etc.
sole   Similar to the floor of a house. The cabin and the cockpit have soles.
sound   To measure water depth with a sounding pole, lead line, or electronic sounding device. Also, to measure contents of a vessel's water tank or bilge.
sounding pole   A hand-held rod with measured marks used to determine water depth.
spade rudder   See **rudder.**
spar   Term for masts, booms, gaffs, or bowsprits.
speak   To raise a vessel or station, generally by hailing or conversing.
speed   See **seas.**

speed logs   Traditional devices and methods for determining speed and distance run. Some are:

chip log   A large chip made fast to the end of a measured and marked line is dropped overboard, and the distance run out in a predetermined number of seconds is counted. Traditionally marked by knots tied every 23.6 feet and run for 14 seconds; each knot run out would represent one knot of speed.

Dutchman's log   A given distance is marked off on the boat, and the crew counts the time it takes the boat to pass a chip dropped from the forward mark and leave it at the after mark. Distance is then converted to knots according to the formula $S = \frac{D}{T}$, where S = speed in knots, D = distance, and T = time.

patent log (taffrail log)   A rotator is towed on a woven line whose other end is attached to a recording instrument on the taffrail.

A full explanation of these and other navigational techniques is given in *Sailing in the Fog* by Roger F. Duncan, a volume in the International Marine Seamanship Series.

spill   Allowing a sail to shake spills the wind from it.

spinnaker   A lightweight, three-cornered sail set flying from a spinnaker pole and controlled with sheets from each clew. Used for running and reaching.

spinnaker

spit   A small projection of land, especially a sand bank.

spitfire   A small jib or storm jib.

splice   See **knots and splices.**

spreader lights   Deck illumination lights attached to the underside of the spreaders.

spreaders (cross-trees)   Horizontal struts attached to the mast on either side to increase the spread, and thus the holding power, of the main shrouds. See **standing rigging.**

spring line See **docklines.**

spring stay See **standing rigging.**

spring tide See **tide.**

sprit A spar that extends from the mast near the tack of a four-cornered sail to the peak.

squall A sudden, violent wind often accompanied by rain.

square knot See **knots and splices.**

square rig See **sailing rigs.**

squaresail See **sail parts.**

stall A sail stalls when it begins to lose wind and no longer acts as an aerodynamic foil.

stanchion Post or similar upright.

stand See **tide.**

standing part (end) The end of a line or fall that is made fast. Opposite of **bitter end.** See **knots and splices.**

standing rigging All rigging and associated hardware that supports the mast, keeps it straight, or provides means to attach certain sails, and is permanently installed.

Clevis pins and cotter rings. Note toggle at upper left.

Shrouds support the mast from side to side. **Upper shrouds** run from **chainplates** at the side of the boat, over horizontal spars, called **spreaders,** to **tangs** or **toggles** near the truck (top) of the mast. **Clevis pins** secure the shrouds, and are held in place by cotter pins or cotter rings. **Lower shrouds** run from chainplates to the mast, just beneath the intersection of the spreaders. On tall masts there may be **intermediate shrouds** between the upper and lower shrouds.

Stays support the mast in a fore-and-aft position. A **backstay** leads aft to prevent forward movement of the

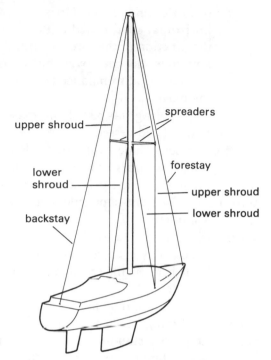

upper shroud

spreaders

lower shroud

forestay

upper shroud

lower shroud

backstay

Standing rigging

mast. A **permanent backstay** runs from masthead to stern. **Running backstays** run from the mast to a point on either quarter, where they are adjusted by winches or levers to keep the windward stay taut and the leeward one loose to avoid interfering with the boom.

A **forestay** leads from the masthead to the bow to prevent backward movement of the mast. If there are two, the forwardmost is the **headstay**. A **jibstay** is the forestay to which the jib is hanked. On a cutter rig, the stay to which a staysail is hanked is the **inner stay,** or **staysail stay.**

On a **masthead rig,** the forestay reaches all the way to the masthead; on a **fractional rig,** it is made fast below the masthead. A **three-quarters rig** attaches at about three-fourths of the distance from the base of the mast, a **seven-eighths rig** at about seven-eights of the distance, and so on. On some fractional rigs a short horizontal spar, called a **jumper strut,** is placed above the junction of the forestay and the mast. On these rigs a **jumper stay** runs over the end of the jumper strut to the masthead to balance the pull of the backstay upon the mast.

A **spring stay** runs from masthead to masthead of a two-masted vessel.

stand-on vessel Under Rules of the Road, the vessel that continues on course while the other vessel gives way. Formerly called the **privileged vessel.**

starboard The right-hand side of a boat when facing the bow. See **port.**

starboard tack See **tack.**

stave A boat has been staved (also stove) when its hull has been broken in, crushed in, or smashed in from the outside.

stays See **standing rigging.**

staysail A triangular headsail hanked to a stay.

staysail stay See **standing rigging.**

steerageway Enough movement through the water for the rudder to act.

stem The most forward part of the bow. Also the foremost upright timber of a wooden boat to which the keel and ends of the planks are attached.

step A recess into which the heel of the mast is placed. Also, to raise and install a mast is to step it.

stern The after (back) end of a boat.

stern anchor See **anchoring.**

stern line A docking line leading from the stern.

stern pulpit See **pulpit.**

stern rail See **pulpit.**

stern sheets The place in the stern of a small open boat not occupied by the thwarts.

stern wave Wave occurring at the stern caused by the motion of the main body of the boat. Also called **quarter wave.**

sternlight   See **navigation lights.**

sternpost   On a wooden vessel, the aftermost timber, reaching from the after end of the keel to the deck, to which the rudder may be fastened. See **rudder.**

sternway   Moving backwards. Opposite of **headway.**

stiff   A boat is stiff when it can carry a relatively large amount of sail without excessive heeling. Otherwise it is **tender.**

stock   The part of a rudder post that passes through the rudder port or tube. See also **anchor.**

stopper knot   Knot tied in the end of a line to prevent it from going through a fairlead or other fitting.

stops   See **sail stops.**

stores   Food stowed for later use.

storm   See **storm warnings.**

storm jib   A small, heavy jib for heavy weather.

storm sails   Small sails for heavy weather sailing.

storm trysail   See **trysail.**

storm warnings   Coastal signals (flags and lights) to warn of wind velocity forecasts as follows: small craft advisory—18–33 knots; gale—34–47 knots; storm—48–63 knots; hurricane—over 63 knots.

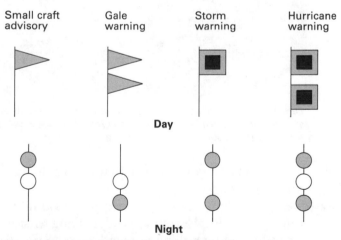

Storm warnings (shaded areas represent red).

stove   See **stave.**

stow   To put gear in its proper place.

strake   A horizontal band of continuous hull planking on a boat.

strut   An external hanger for the shaft of an inboard engine. See **shaft.**

stuffing box (also **packing gland**)   A fitting in the hull through which a shaft or a rudder post projects. It alleviates friction by using packing material and water seepage instead of bearings and grease.

swage   A mechanical method of securing an eye or other fitting to the butt end of a wire.

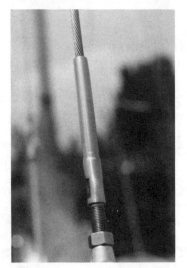 

Left: Fitting with threaded stud on bottom end is swaged onto a shroud, which extrudes from the top. *Right:* Nicopress swage forms an eye around a thimble at the end of a wire.

swamp   To fill a boat with water so that it partially submerges or sinks.

sway (sweat)   To haul tight, generally by making a half or round turn with the running end, placing tension on the standing end by pulling perpendicular to the direction of strain, then quickly exploiting the slack gained by transferring it through the running end. Used to tighten halyards, docklines, etc.

swells   See **seas.**

swing keel   A weighted extension of the keel that can be retracted or locked in the fully lowered position.

swing ship (swing compass)   To swing ship is to move the boat through the compass points to check the magnetic compass on different headings, note the deviation, and prepare a deviation card.

tabernacle   A hinged socket where the base of the mast fits, to enable the mast to be raised or lowered.

tabling   See **sail parts.**

tachometer   An instrument for counting the revolutions of a motor.

tack   To come about, or turn the bow of a boat through the wind so that it then blows across the opposite side. A boat is on a **port tack** when the wind is blowing on the port side of the mainsail, causing the main boom to be on the starboard side. A **starboard tack** is the opposite. See also **sail parts.**

tackle   A purchase system using ropes and blocks, which is used to gain a mechanical advantage. Often pronounced "tay-kle."

taffrail   See **pulpit.**

taffrail log   See **speed logs.**

tail   A crewmember tails by hauling in on a line leading to a winch.

tang   A fitting on a spar to which standing rigging is secured.

telltale   A small length of wool or other material attached to a sail near the luff or leech to make the pattern of air flow over the sail visible, to aid in trimming the sail properly. Often called **luff-woolly** if on the luff.

tender   A small boat or dinghy used to provide transportation services for a yacht. Also, a sailboat that heels easily in the wind. Opposite of **stiff.**

tether   A line, often attached to a safety harness, that keeps a person on board, or if in the water keeps him from being lost astern.

Tether attached to a safety harness.

thimble   A metal or plastic loop around which a line is tied, spliced, or seized to form a hard eye.

The bight at the end of this anchor rode has been spliced around a thimble. Splice has been seized. Rode will be attached to anchor or chain by shackle at left.

three-quarters rig   See **standing rigging.**

throat   See **sail parts.**

through-hull fitting (thru hull)   Tubular hardware affixed to a hole drilled in the hull to which intake and discharge hoses, cockpit and cabin drains, impellers, transducers, etc., can be attached. Kept watertight by a seacock, ball cock, gate valve, or through-hull cap or plug.

A **seacock** is a valve that controls the flow of water by means of an internal channelized ball operated by an external lever. It is generally considered to be the safest type of valve. A **ball cock** is similar to a seacock. A **gate valve** operates like a home water faucet.

Lever turned parallel to ball cock fitting, left, is in open position. Turning it 90 degrees will close it. Gate valve, right, is partly closed; its handle must be screwed down clockwise if it is to be fully closed.

thwart   A seat or brace running across a boat.

thwartships   See **athwartships.**

tidal current   The horizontal flow of water caused by variations in tide height. Current moving toward land is **flooding,** moving away from land is **ebbing,** and unmoving is **slack.** Current is measured by **set,** which is the direction toward which the current is flowing, and **drift,** which is its speed in knots.

tide   The vertical movement of water caused by sun, moon, and the earth's rotation. **Range** is the vertical distance between high and low tides in a given area. **Rise** is the height difference between low water and the sea surface at any time. Tide **stands** when no vertical move-

tide

ment is taking place. **Mean high tides** and **mean low tides** are average measurements for a given area, and can be exceeded during **spring tides,** which are the highest high tides, and the lowest low tides, that occur twice a lunar month during the full and new moons. **Neap tides,** which rise and fall the least from the average level (have the least range), occur during the moon's first and third quarters.

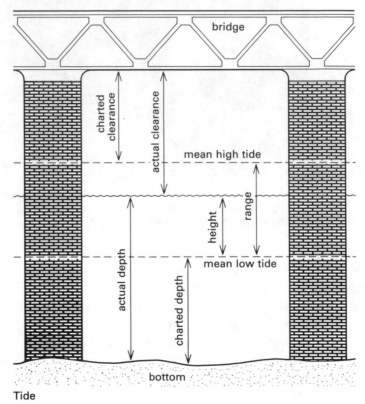

Tide

tide-rip   Rough water caused by action of the tide over the bottom. See also **race.**

tide-rode A boat is tide-rode when it is facing into the tidal stream when anchored or at a mooring. Opposite of **wind-rode**.

tiller An arm on the rudder post to control the rudder. See illustration for **rudder.**

time/distance formula See **D = ST.**

toggle An end fitting to standing or running rigging, generally attached to a tang or clevis with a clevis pin, secured by a cotter ring or cotter pin to hold it in place.

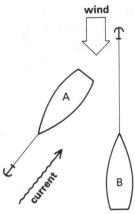

Boat A is tide-rode. Boat B is wind-rode.

topping lift A tackle, rope, or cable used to support the boom when it is not supported by a raised sail. See **boom crotch.**

topside (topsides) The side of a boat between the waterline and the deck. Also on deck.

towboat (tug) A vessel especially designed to tow or push another vessel.

towline Line used to tow another vessel or boat. Big towboats use towing **hausers.**

track Railing or slot along which a mainsailor a trysail can be hoisted or lowered, or along which a sheet block can be moved for adjusting headsail sheets. See also **dead reckoning.**

transducer An electronic sounding device that transmits sound to the bottom and times the echo for depth determination.

transom The thwartships, flat-
tened part of the stern.

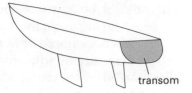

transom

transverse At right angles to
the centerline.

trapeze A support used by the
crew of a racing dinghy
to enable them to place
their weight outside the
boat.

traveler (traveller, horse) See **running rigging.**

trim Fore-and-aft or thwartships balance of the boat. To trim
sails is to adjust them for the apparent wind and desired direction of sail.

trip A boat trips when her bow digs into a sea.

trip line See **anchoring.**

trough See **seas.**

true wind See **wind.**

trunk The structure that houses a
centerboard.

trysail (storm trysail) A triangular
loose-footed sail fitted aft
of the mast and used to re-
place the mainsail in heavy
weather. It can be fitted on
the mainsail track, or on a
separate trysail track.

Storm trysail and working jib

tug See **towboat.**

tumblehome The inward curve of
a vessel's sides. The reverse
of **flare.**

turn See **knots and splices.**

turn of the bilge The lower outer part of the hull where it
turns from the vertical and rounds to meet the keel.

turn turtle See **capsize.**

turnbuckle (bottlescrew) A fitting to adjust tension on standing rigging, threaded right-handed on one end and left-handed on the other. One end of the wire cable normally has a swaged stud that screws into a turnbuckle.

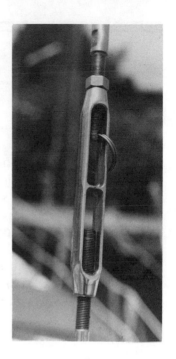

The wire cable is held securely in place by the nut atop the turnbuckle and the cotter ring inserted through a hole in the stud. Safety could be enhanced by a cotter pin or second cotter ring through the bottom stud.

turning block A block used to change the direction of a line such as a halyard or sheet.

turtle A bag used for folding and deploying a spinnaker.

two-block To draw the two blocks of a tackle as close together as possible.

unbend   To cast off or untie, especially to detach a sail from its spar or stay.

underway   The condition of a boat that is not moored, anchored, or aground.

unfurl   To cast loose a sail for raising.

Universal Time   See **Greenwich Meridian.**

unreeve   The opposite of **reeve.**

up and down   The condition of an anchor rode that is vertical, preparatory to breaking out the anchor.

upper shrouds   See **standing rigging.**

upwind   To windward, toward the wind.

vang   A tackle or line used to prevent a gaff or sprit from sagging to leeward. See **boom vang.**

variation   See **compass.**

vector diagram   A graphic method of determining a third variable by geometrically applying two known variables. Vector diagrams are used to calculate set and drift, or to determine a course to compensate for set and drift. They are also used to find true wind from boat speed and apparent wind; or apparent wind from boat speed and true wind. Vector diagrams also disclose the relative speed of two vessels closing with each other.

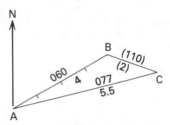

Using a vector diagram to calculate set and drift

Starting from a known position, you motor on course 060 at 4 knots (course and speed through the water), and obtain a fix exactly 1 hour later. Plotting the fix on the chart (see illustration for **dead reckoning**) discloses that you have traveled 5.5 nautical miles along a bearing of 077 degrees. This is a course and speed made good. To calculate your set and drift: 1. Make a scale of convenient length. 2. Draw a vertical line representing north. 3. Using the scale and a protractor, draw line A-B (060 degrees, 4 nautical miles), representing course and speed through the water for 1 hour. 4. Draw a line A-C (077 degrees, 5.5 nautical miles), starting at the known position (A), and ending at the fix (B). This is course and speed made good over the ground. 5. Construct line B-C. Its angular measurement from north is set (110 degrees); its length measured on the scale is drift (2 knots).

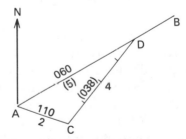

Using a vector diagram to compensate for set and drift

Assume you want to make good a course of 060 degrees, and you intend to motor at 4 knots. You estimate that the set and drift you determined from the preceding example will continue to be

110 degrees and 2 knots respectively. To find the course to steer: 1. Use a convenient scale, and draw a north line. 2. Draw line A-B (060 degrees) for any convenient distance. This is the desired track (course to be made good). 3. Draw line A-C, representing set (110 degrees) and drift (2 knots) for 1 hour. 4. Construct line C-D by measuring 4 nautical miles on the scale with dividers, and transferring that measurement to run from C, to where it just touches line A-B, and draw C-D. The angular measurement of C-D from north is the course to steer (038 degrees). The length of A-D measured on the scale is speed over the ground (5 knots).

veer   To let out more scope on an anchor rode. See also **wind.**

vessel (craft)   Any large boat or ship.

wake   A boat's visible track through the water trailing out astern. Consists of the turbulence caused by the boat's passage through the water.

wake course   The bearing of the wake relative to the boat's heading, which assists in determining leeway. See **dead reckoning.**

warp   To move a vessel by lines (warps). Also a long heavy line streamed astern to slow the boat's speed when running under bare poles, or streamed to slow movement when hove-to or lying-to.

washboards (dropboards)   Boards used to close the vertical opening in a companionway hatch.

waterline   A line painted on the side of a boat to show loading capacity and to aid in achieving proper trim. See **boot stripe.**

waves   See **seas.**

way   Movement of a boat through the water such as headway, sternway, or leeway. If the boat is moving, it has **way on.**

wear   To put the stern through the wind. See **jibe.**

weather   See **windward.**

weather deck   The topside deck exposed to wind and seas.

weather helm   A boat has weather helm when it heads up, or turns to weather with its helm free. A slight weather helm is normally preferred for safety. Opposite of **lee helm.** See also **center of effort.**

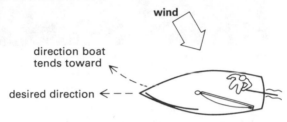

In a boat with weather helm, the rudder must be held off-center to counterbalance the boat's tendency to turn into the wind.

weather shore   The land to windward of a boat. Opposite of **lee shore.**

weigh anchor   To lift the anchor from the bottom.

well-found   A vessel that is well equipped.

wharf   A structure bounding the edge of a dock and built along or at an angle to the shoreline, used for loading and unloading cargo and passengers.

wheel   Used in place of a tiller to steer a larger boat.

whip   To bind the ends of a rope with small stuff, tape, or plastic, to prevent fraying. The ends of nylon and dacron ropes may also be fused by heat or coated with special liquids to avoid fraying.

whisker pole   Any spar used to extend the jib when running, or sometimes when on a broad reach.

winch

winch A drum trimmed by a crank or by power used to provide mechanical advantage when raising or trimming sails.

Winch

wind The initiating force for sail propulsion. **True wind** is the direction from which the wind is blowing. Its speed and direction can be perceived from a stationary object. **Wind of motion** derives from the movement of the boat. True wind and wind of motion combine to produce **apparent wind,** which is perceived when sailing.

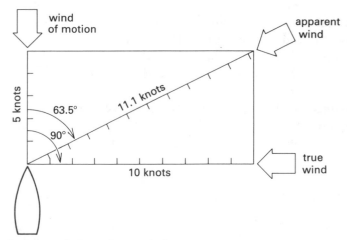
Apparent wind on a beam reach.

Relative wind is the direction of the apparent wind relative to the boat's bow.

Apparent wind is always forward of the true wind (except when true wind is dead ahead or dead astern). Thus, if boat speed and one wind are known, the other wind can be calculated from a vector diagram.

Wind **veers** if it changes direction clockwise and **backs** if it changes direction counterclockwise. **Gradient wind** blows from high pressure to low pressure above the influence of land or water.

Buys Ballot's Law states that if you stand with your back to the wind, you will have low pressure on your left-hand side in the northern hemisphere.

wind of motion See **wind.**

wind vane The part of a self-steering system that responds to the wind, causing the rudder to steer a fixed course relative to the wind. Also a pointer fixed at the top of the mast to indicate relative wind direction.

windlass See **capstan.**

wind-rode A boat is wind-rode when it is facing into the wind when anchored or at a mooring. Opposite of **tide-rode.**

windward (pronounced "winderd") The weather side, or side toward the wind. Opposite of **leeward.**

wing-and-wing (butterfly) Running with the mainsail set on one side of the boat and the jib set on the other. Also applied to running with two headsails, one set on either side.

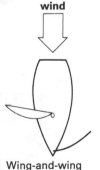

wind

Wing-and-wing

wire Safety wire is used to keep shackle pins secure. Multi-stranded wire is used for stays, shrouds, and sometimes halyards.

working jib A general-purpose jib, generally with an area of from 75 to 100 percent of the foretriangle.

working sails Used for general purpose under normal conditions. On a sloop, the mainsail and a jib.

yard A horizontal spar from which a square sail is suspended.
yardarm The extremities of a yard.
yaw A boat's motion around a vertical axis.
yawl See **sailing rigs.**

zincs Sacrificial fittings installed around shafts, near propellers, inside salt-water–cooled engines, and other places where needed to protect against electrolysis.

Zinc is bolted around the shaft, to the right of the strut.